An Angel
at my
Shoulder

An Angel
at my
Shoulder

*True stories of
angelic experiences*

by
Glennyce S. Eckersley

RIDER
LONDON • SYDNEY • AUCKLAND • JOHANNESBURG

First published in 1996

1 3 5 7 9 10 8 6 4 2

Published in 1996 by Rider,
an imprint of Ebury Press, Random House,
20 Vauxhall Bridge Road, London SW1V 2SA

Random House Australia (Pty) Limited
20 Alfred Street, Milsons Point, Sydney, New South Wales 2061, Australia

Random House New Zealand Limited
18 Poland Road, Glenfield, Auckland 10, New Zealand

Random House South Africa (Pty) Limited
PO Box 337, Bergvlei 2012, South Africa

Random House UK Limited Reg. No. 954009

Papers used by Rider Books are natural, recyclable products made
from wood grown in sustainable forests. In addition, the paper in this
book is acid-free.

Typeset by SX Composing DTP, Rayleigh, Essex.
Printed by Cox & Wyman

A CIP catalogue record for this book is available from the British Library.

ISBN 0-7126-7208-7

To Gillian and Rachel
a pair of grounded angels

*I am well aware of the fact that
many people will say that nobody can possibly
speak to spirits or angels as long as he is living
in the body, and that many will call it delusion.
Some will say that I have spread these ideas
around so as to win people's trust, while others
will say something different again.
But none of this deters me;
for I have seen; I have heard;
I have felt.*

EMANUEL SWEDENBORG
(from *Arcana Caelestia* – Heavenly Secrets)

Contents

Preface

In recent years there has been an enormous upsurge of interest in angels and angelic activity. This has been fuelled by the experiences of thousands of people who have felt an angelic presence in their lives, seen visions and experienced life-changing encounters. This is not a new phenomenon, but previously people tended to keep their experiences to themselves. Nowadays there is more openness to the dimensions of the mysterious and the spiritual, so more people are telling their moving and dramatic stories. As public interest increases, so hunger grows to know more about these mysterious beings of light, bringers of comfort.

For some years, there have been reports from America that many people are experiencing contact with angels, and at least one angel 'network' has been formed to make people aware of the widespread nature of this phenomenon. Once my own curiosity had been aroused, I became keenly interested to discover if people in Britain and other countries were also experiencing angel encounters. Perhaps they were keeping them to themselves for fear of being laughed at.

My extensive research makes it clear that angels are appearing all over the world as well as in the USA. There are, however, certain differences. A larger number of the American experiences strongly feature a 'dramatic rescue' scenario, whereas more of the stories revealed to me, particularly in Britain, deal with a gentler type of encounter. In this sort of experience, feelings and light are often more prominent than visions of angels. Near-death experiences are now more generally accepted and bear strong resemblances to angelic encounters, making them currently more widely discussed.

The question remains: why now? Why the intense interest in everything to do with angels — books, art, films and so on? Could it be that for several decades materialism and enthusiasm for all things secular have dominated, leaving a spiritual wilderness and a large gap and sense of loss in people's lives? Could it be that the spiritual wavelengths are once more being tuned into, and people are now receiving? After decades of material plenty, in certain parts of the globe at least, could we at last be learning the importance of love?

Many people find in retrospect that events that seemed inexplicable at the time can later be understood as angelic intervention. This is certainly true of my own experience which, compared to the stories told in this book, was very modest.

One winter evening a sequence of events took place as I was sitting with a close friend, catching up with each other's news. Chatting gave us a sense of well-being and, because of our involvement with young people, we discussed the positive feedback received by giving them attention and love. We talked a great deal and drank numerous cups of tea before arriving at the conclusion that love was not only the most important aspect of our lives, but the very reason for them. Counting blessings for all the love surrounding us, the very special people close to us and the love and respect we held for each other, we suddenly became aware of several changes in the room. At precisely the same moment we each experienced a tingling sensation from head to toe, closely followed by an awareness that the light in the room had increased. Starting from a single point at floor level, it spread into a diffuse glow that filled the whole room. The atmosphere was one of peace, love and intense happiness. We were lost for words but agreed there had been a presence and a vis-itation of some kind, the nature of which we could only guess at. A very positive outlook, and a reaching for-ward, has remained with me since that time – as well as a knowledge of things yet to be achieved. Many explanations could be offered but, personally, I believe in angels.

There is no doubt that this experience made me feel

I had something particular to do, that some challenge awaited me. It seemed I had only to wait and listen to discover what this challenge was and, looking back now, I can see that I have been gently, imperceptibly led on a journey towards contemporary accounts of angels by people who wanted to share them. This involved extensive research, including meetings, interviews and telephone conversations with over one hundred people.

I have been deeply moved by the accounts I heard, related to me with such trust and honesty. People were often in tears as they recalled these events, but insisted the story be told as an example to others, and in many cases for the sheer relief of telling their story for the first time. Some names have been changed at the request of those who wished it. It was a very powerful experience listening to people's accounts of what had happened to them, and I have tried to keep that effect in this book. A few have sent in their own versions of their experiences, but in most cases I have written up their stories from what they told me, keeping some sections in the first person.

I should like at this point to say a huge thank you to David Lomax, Ian Arnold and Michael Stanley for all their help, advice and encouragement with this book. For their written ideas and information, plus moral and practical support in abundance, they have my thanks, and without these three special people this book would not have happened.

Thank you to Judith Kendra, my editor, who has, from the start, wanted the angel of fun to be part of this project.

A final thank you to contributors for their generosity and willingness to share such very personal experiences. There would not have been a book without them. They have all been left with the feeling that the angels are ever-present to help and comfort. Their names are: John Marsh, Lorna Kenyon, Andrew Stockley, Bishop Alexis Bilindabagabo, Inelia Avila, Elizabeth Brown, Sharif Gulsher, Mary Buckingham, Ann Wheeler, Pam Cuthbert, George, Millie Jaum, Lilian Ainscow, Kate Geers, Mavis Croft, William Thaw, Sarah Morton, Jean Smith, Helen O'Connor, Janice O'Gara, Elizabeth Derbyshire, Jean Jael, Sylvia Swinfield, Hazel Raven, Robert Haseler, Avril Makin, Jo Whittier-Marshall, Dominic March, David Glover, Leopold Hubert Bauer, John Michaelson, Richard Hearmon, Claire Brown, Carole Pearson, Karen Scott, Graham Taylor, Mike White, Elsie Dow, Susan Caulfield, Paniyota Peppos, Janet Murray, Jonathan Scott, Jean Earl, Kate Ells, Jonathan Haulgrave, Stephanie Hanley, Tim, Julie Blinston, Leah Clarkson, Di Cecil-Clarke, Grace Rigby, Rebekah Rigby, David Rigby, Judith Horridge, Betty Johnson, Ian Arnold, Janet Bull, Natalie White, Dorothea Hutchison, Stella Sillett, Peter Hague, Donna Barker, Andrew Greenhalgh, Mary Hargreaves.

I hope that *An Angel at My Shoulder* speaks to you, and

leads you too along angelic pathways. I would like to conclude this preface with a misquotation of a popular saying: 'An Angel is for Life, not just for Christmas'.

1

Who are Angels?

Stories of angels are found in the scriptures of all the world's religions and mythologies, and images of these gracious winged comforters abound in the art of every great culture, from the massive winged beasts of stone in ancient Persia and Egypt to the delicate miniatures of the Renaissance. But who are these mysterious beings? They come and go, in and out of consciousness and fashion, leaving little trace apart from their indelible impact upon the lives of those they touch.

We do not know the origins of angels, who seem to have been with us always, well before the beginning of recorded history. In Western civilisation, they are encountered throughout the Old Testament, being featured in about 300 stories. Christianity took them over, developing an elaborate angel lore of systems, hierarchies, roles and duties, which reached its peak in the Middle Ages, in the *Summa Theologica* of Thomas Aquinas. This period also produced the greatest flowering of angelic art, when thousands of exquisitely beautiful images graced the paintings of the

Renaissance artists, the stained-glass windows and frescoes of the churches. Angels waned in popularity with the rise of science, which provided more materialistic explanations for the order of the world, but they never disappeared from view entirely.

In the eighteenth century, one of the most detailed theories of angels was developed by the Swedish scientist and philosopher Emanuel Swedenborg. In midlife he became increasingly aware of angel realms, and for 27 years had personal contact and conversations with angels, who revealed to him many aspects of the spiritual world. Out of his extensive experience and studies he wrote many books (some of which are listed in the further reading list at the back of this book). One of his unique contributions to angel lore was the theory that human beings are all born with an inner angelic nature, which can easily become forgotten or hidden but is always waiting to be discovered. He believed that the souls of people who have previously lived on earth and are now close to God may become angels, who are there to help us in our spiritual development through 'angel-to-angel' contact. Some of these ideas inspired the artist and poet William Blake, who created many of the most beautiful images of angels in Western art, and featured angels in his poetic mythology.

The greatest revival of interest in angels since the Renaissance was in the Victorian age, when angels reappeared in poetry, hymns and painting, particularly in Pre-Raphaelite art, and angel monuments proliferated in the cemeteries. This was the beginning of their prevalence in popular culture, which has never diminished, until today they are found in the modern media of films, and popular music, as well as being the favourite motif of Christmas cards.

The First World War was the height of angel sightings. Previously, at least since the Middle Ages, such sightings had been private affairs communicated only to family, if at all. But in the mass slaughter of trench warfare such stories became more public and even commonplace, including the most famous account of the Angel of Mons, in which a whole troop of angels was witnessed by many British soldiers, who attributed their escape from massacre by the Germans to their apparent intervention. This period abounds with many such stories. As we will see, intervention and rescue at times of crisis and tragedy is the main angelic function in this world.

After the First World War, not much was heard of angels for a long time, except at Christmas. Now they have suddenly made a reappearance on an unprecedented scale, in the lives of the thousands of people who have encountered them, and in the even greater numbers of people with no personal experience but who nevertheless believe in them and long to develop their own capacities to see these beings and receive their help. But to return to our original question: who are angels? Do we know any more of their function and role in our lives?

THE HEAVENLY ORDER OF ANGELS

The word 'angel' means messenger, and in religions that feature angels they are described as messengers and intermediaries between God and humanity. As mentioned, Christian theologians created an elaborate hierarchy ranking the angels from those closest to God to those who spend more time with humanity. The most widely accepted system of classification is the sixth century 'Pseudo Dionysius' theory of nine celestial orders or choirs, divided into three triads. The first triad consists of Seraphim, Cherubim and Thrones. These have the highest rate of vibration, and they spend their time circling the highest point or centre of the cosmos – the divine core, Throne of Glory, God, or whatever term one wishes to use. The second triad consists of Dominions, Virtues and Powers, whose rate of vibration is slightly lower, closer to matter. Above this triad all is unity, oneness, but at this point duality arises with the beginning of division into good and bad, matter and spirit, higher and lower. Finally we come to the third triad: Principalities, Archangels and Angels. These are closer in vibration to the physical world, hence more able to interact with and help humanity.

Angels, and occasionally Archangels, are the beings most likely to be encountered in angelic visitations, although some people refer to their visitors as 'cherubs', perhaps because cherubs are so often (misleadingly!) depicted on church ceilings and greetings cards as cuddly child angels. The most popular of all subtypes of angel is the guardian angel. In the past, whole nations believed themselves under the protection of a guardian angel. Some religions believe we all have one or more personal angels allotted to us at birth, to act as spiritual guardians, watching over us and preserving us from harm. Even if we do not see or acknowledge them, they are active on our behalf, steering us away from accidents or misfortune, comforting us in grief and bereavement. Sometimes when people realize their lucky escape, they attribute it to the intervention of their guardian angel, even when there has been no overt sign or sighting. In addition, it seems that guardian angels may function as spiritual guides, giving us access to our own wisdom and other spiritual sources of knowledge and wisdom. Some mediums and channels claim to be helped in this way by their guardian angels.

Although many angels have names, these are not generally known, and only two are named in the Bible, the Archangels Michael and Gabriel, although others are well known from the apocrypha, such as Raphael and Uriel. Michael in particular is the angel most likely to be recognised and named in people's accounts, particularly if the angel encountered is bearing a sword, which is how Michael is often depicted. There are many stories of his heroic exploits on behalf of humanity. He is known as the greatest of all angels, and is sometimes seen as God's great champion, the Prince of Light leading the fight against the forces of darkness. He is also the original slayer of the dragon in that legend and is often depicted in this capacity, wielding his sword.

WHAT DO ANGELS LOOK LIKE?

Angels are seen and experienced by human beings in many different guises. A few of the stories in this book describe angels reminiscent of the medieval knight, complete with sword and breastplate. However, most people describe their angels as less martial, closer to the exquisite, ethereal beings depicted in Renaissance and pre-Raphaelite art. Whatever form they take, they are often literally larger than life. Medieval theologians debated the famous question 'How many angels can dance on a pinhead?', but often angels fill the whole room with their presence, even overflow its boundaries, their feet reaching through the floor, their heads soaring through the ceiling. Interestingly, they are often of indeterminate gender, which accords with the theological definition of angels as androgynous. This is mainly how they are depicted in art, although child angels were usually male, and Pre-Raphaelite art often portrayed female angels. Some accounts, however, do describe the angel as either male or female. Their androgynous appearance is partly due

12

to their clothing; they are usually seen as dressed in long, flowing robes. The colours vary, but the style is consistent.

The most spectacular aspect of their appearance is the bright glow that invariably emanates from them. Few people mention the halo that surrounds their heads in most paintings, probably because the light is so dazzling (though not blinding) that it surrounds their entire form, sometimes filling the whole room with radiance. Their features are often perceived only dimly through this luminescence, though people are sometimes struck by the intensity of angels' eyes, which may blaze with light and fire. Their eyes are sometimes perceived as blue, while their hair may be blond and curly, but these features if noted at all do vary considerably, and may owe something to popular art. Of course, wings are the most dramatic tribute of the angel, marking them off from other spiritual beings – although they are not remarked on by all witnesses. When they are present they are usually large, often white though sometimes multi-coloured, and may also gently enfold those in need of comfort and reassurance.

BRINGERS OF COMFORT AND PEACE

Comfort and reassurance are the key qualities that emerge from people's own experiences of angels. Occasionally the first reaction may be fear, often the result of astonishment at such a strange and unexpected appearance. But this feeling is nearly always swiftly overtaken by solace and peace, as the healing effects of the visitation manifest. Such healing is often urgently required, for the most common occurrences of these incidents are at times of great need and crisis. As we shall see, angels are kept busy visiting sickbeds, comforting the lonely, the dying and the bereaved. They may intervene with an unseen hand on the shoulder to stop a child walking down a dangerous path, or even with a powerful yank on the shoulder to prevent a child running across a busy main road. Yet angels may also be playful, even humorous, and their light touch may help us lighten up our own lives. Their effect is always positive and inspiring. Some people are visited more than once, perhaps whenever they face a crisis. A few are even continuously aware of angelic presences, who become a familiar part of their life like friends or 'elder brothers and sisters. Whether we encounter them once only or many times, they leave a vivid, indelible impression that reverberates throughout our lives and may sometimes dramatically change the whole course of our life for the better.

But now it is time to turn to the accounts themselves, the true stories of men, women and children leading outwardly normal lives, but who have been touched by the wing of an angel, comforted, inspired, uplifted and transformed, and whose experience is relevant to us all.

Angels to the Rescue

They will lift you in their hands,
so that you will not strike your foot
against a stone.

PSALM 91

Most people think of angels as beings who rescue us from danger, and this seems to be a highly significant angelic function, one which is bound to capture our attention. It is, of course, only one of the areas in which they help human beings, but I have received many dramatic accounts of people whose lives have been saved by angels.

Donna's story is one of these. She had been invited to a 21st birthday party by an old schoolfriend. The party was to be held in late November at an exclusive restaurant, beginning with cocktails at 6.30, followed by dinner with a live band. Donna had bought a new dress and shoes for the occasion, and was trying them on with great pleasure. To complete her excitement, she had a new boyfriend who was going to escort her to the party in his car.

They both chatted happily as they drove towards the

party, while Donna read the map. They were heading for Bristol, a city in the south-west of England which Michael had never visited before. All went well until they had almost reached the city's suburbs, when they realized they must have taken a wrong turning. Donna felt Michael was driving too fast and had shot past the turning before she could stop him. She stayed calm, not wanting to spoil the happy mood, but it was soon clear that they were lost. It was now getting dark and late. They stopped and studied the map, trying to work out a short cut back to the main road. Off they roared, down a narrow lane and under a bridge, driving even faster to make up for lost time. Suddenly the road took a sharp left turn and, to their horror, they saw a large van ahead of them parked right on the bend.

The events of the next few seconds seemed to happen in slow motion. There was a sharp sound of metal hitting metal, Michael was yelling, and Donna was aware only of a bright light surrounding her. Through the windscreen she saw, not the stationary vehicle, but a bright, shining figure surrounded by a light so strong she could not find words to describe it. A beautiful face gazed at her through the window. Then everything went blank, and the next event Donna remembered was being lifted into a hospital bed.

Michael's only injury was whiplash and Donna had a broken leg. However the car was concertinaed into waves of metal, including the passenger seat. The van they had hit was also completely crushed. No one could explain how Donna had been in the passenger seat yet escaped with her life. Members of the ambulance crew said it was as if she had been in a protective bubble, with just enough space to protect her while everything around her crumpled.

Donna cannot begin to understand what happened that night. However, she is certain that the vision of the figure in front of the car at the moment of impact was no dream. She feels it could only have been her guardian angel, and who are we to disagree?

Then there is John's story. Meeting an angel was particularly dramatic for him, and as with so many dramatic experiences it took place at a time of great crisis. The build-up to that event goes back a long way, to John's childhood. Growing up had not been easy for him, with very little money to spare for treats or holidays, and everything in the family having to be shared, from the few toys in the house to clothes and even shoes. He grew tired of wishing for a football or, even more impossible, a bike. Small items that most children took for granted, like marbles or a penknife, were also out of his reach. Eventually, his desire to have something which belonged exclusively to him grew so strong that he stole from a shop. Soon John was stealing on a regular basis. As his confidence in his ability not to be caught grew, so his thefts became bolder and he started to break into people's houses.

Then, when John reached twenty, without a job and involved in a life of petty crime, something marvellous happened – he met a girl who was pretty, caring, witty and wonderful. Soon John was head over heels in love. She worked as a clerk in a large local electrical company and, to John's amazement, returned his love. For the first time in many years John now began to feel ashamed of his life and vowed to change, to 'clean up his act' and start a fresh chapter with his new love, Helen.

Months passed and one day, having applied for many jobs, he was successful in being given one in a garage. He was determined to work hard and learn as much as he possibly could about the motor trade. A year passed and John was feeling very proud of himself. He had an aptitude for the work and so, feeling very happy and content, he asked Helen to marry him. When she said yes to his proposal John felt that, if he was to embark on this new life, he must tell Helen all his guilty secrets, wipe the slate clean and start with a clear conscience.

Helen, though shocked, forgave him, but made him promise never to keep anything from her in future and never to stray from the straight and narrow. They married and rented a little house on the edge of the small town in which they both worked. John wanted Helen to have the best of everything, but setting up house was much more expensive than either had imagined. Helen did not complain and appeared happy enough, but

John's old feeling, which had tortured him so as a child, returned – why should they be without and have to struggle?

A day came when the inevitable happened. He saw his employer place a large strong-box of money in his desk drawer with the intention of banking it later in the day. While talking business in the car yard the boss left the office empty for a while and, forgetting all reason, John took the money and fled. Just where he was going and what he was doing he did not know. He even took a car from the garage forecourt, which compounded his stupidity. He had been driving for what seemed like hours when the adrenalin finally stopped racing through his veins and the enormity of the crime hit him. He could not possibly get away with it, he had gone back on his promise to himself and, worse still, he had let down his beloved Helen.

At this point he realised that he was near the coast and it came to him in his despair that the only course of action left to him would be to go over a cliff and end it all. It was growing dark when he reached the cliff. Shaking, he wrote a brief note for Helen, apologising for everything, and then, leaving the car and the strong-box, he walked to the top of the cliffs, preparing himself to jump. The drop was indeed steep enough to kill him, the tide was in and very deep and John knew that it would be the end of him the minute he left the cliff-top.

Suddenly a light filled the air around him. It

encircled him completely and, directly in front of him, a figure appeared in outline, huge and shining, with wings that bent forward to encircle him. No words were spoken, but there was a powerful feeling of love and protection. John stood rooted to the spot, feeling no fear but knowing instantly that he must go back and face the music, no matter what. The vision gradually faded as the light slowly moved away over the sea, but the powerful feeling stayed with him.

He went back to find his employer and told him the whole story. His boss was furious and raged at John, but several days later relented and gave him another chance. Helen, too, was devastated at first but she eventually relented and also gave John a second chance. Today, ten years on, they own a house, beautifully and honestly furnished. John told me he will never steal again for, to this day, he feels the effects of that angelic experience.

John's account is dramatic and moving, complete with a fully visible angel and a circle of light. It is useful to note at this point, however, that rescues can be just as spectacular without these visual aspects. In some ways Lorna's story is even more gripping for having none of these. She remembers the period in her life when she and her teenage son seemed to be clashing on a regular basis, especially regarding the time to return home at night. At 14 years old, Michael was as tall as his father and bitterly resented a 10 p.m. curfew.

He felt like a man and thought his mother was a fussy old hen. She would worry when he was late, especially as he would frequently cycle home without his bicycle lights and protective clothing. Lorna was sure that this was not done deliberately to annoy or worry her, but Michael was in such a rush to meet his friends at the beginning of the evening that preparations for the return journey did not enter his head.

One night, late in winter, Michael had gone to a friend's to play records and as usual all thoughts of time left his head. When 10.30 arrived, Lorna rang his friend's to remind him to come home, but was told he had started for home just minutes before. His lights and reflective strip sat on a chair in the hall, and out-side it was now very dark indeed. Worried, she tried to calculate how long it would take him, and began to pace anxiously. Sipping tea and feeling the rising panic, she was at a loss to know what to do. Her husband was away from home in the car, so she was unable to find him and put his bike on top of the car. Minutes seemed like hours, until Michael finally burst through the kitchen door, ashen-faced and trembling. All thoughts of chastisement left her as she rushed towards him. She hugged him closely and realised to her surprise he was hugging her back twice as hard.

Michael then told her the following story. 'Realising how late I was, and knowing I was in trouble, especially if the police spotted me without lights, I decided to take a quicker, quieter route along the canal tow-path.

Almost at once I knew I had made a stupid decision as the path was ill-lit and very rough, so I found my bike bouncing around and coming dangerously close to the foul-looking water. Too scared to get off and walk, for the place looked so eerie at night, I tried to pedal faster. My heart was pounding and I was very conscious of the wall which fell away steeply to the canal on my left, especially as I am a very poor swimmer. Perspiration trickled down my back with fear. Suddenly, I felt the handlebars of my bike turn severely to the right, forcing me to ride into the side of a bank with such speed that I went up it a little way, before descending again to the path some yards ahead. The bike was not under my control, I merely sat with my hands holding the handlebars, being directed by the force. At last I reached the end of the tow-path and was once more on a road with lighting, feeling safe. I stopped pedalling to catch my breath, my heart still beating strongly, and tried to work out what had happened. At this point, a neighbour appeared, walking the family dog. Recognising me, he said, "What are you doing? Isn't it time you were home?" Seeing I had no lights, he said, "I'll walk back with you. You'd be better off pushing your bike without lights. And it's a good job you didn't take the tow-path." When I asked why, he said that a large hole had appeared about half way along the path due to a collapsed drain, dangerous in day-time, but lethal at night.'

The unseen hands which seized Michael's handlebars had clearly steered him around that gaping hole. He may not have seen lights or white wings, but surely he had been saved by an angel that night.

An angel also made its presence felt to prevent another bike accident, this time with a motor-bike. This story was told to me by a friend who experienced the event many years ago. He was driving his motor-bike, attached to which was a side-car in which his long-suffering wife was sitting. She felt very nervous and vulnerable in the side-car, but this was their only means of transport. Bowling along at top speed and tearing round a sharp bend, my friend heard a very loud voice bellow, 'Stop!' Slamming on his brakes and stopping as quickly as humanly possible, he was horrified to see his front wheel leave the bike and career down a precipitous bank. Shaken, he looked around, but no one was in sight and he knew that the voice was too loud to have been human. His guardian angel had certainly served him well on that occasion.

We can already see that angels rescue people in different ways, but can they rescue more than one person in a dangerous predicament? Maybe even dozens of people? It seems they can, and this next account is remarkable because it was witnessed by many people. It happened when Andrew was 15 years of age and accompanying his parents on a visit to Lee Abbey in Devon, England. The Abbey is an old and beautiful building, an Anglican retreat centre set amongst fields and occupied by monks. The grounds of the Abbey contain chalets for visitors' use, and it was in one of these chalets that Andrew and his family were staying. Immediately behind the chalet was a 60-foot cliff, on top of which an extensive car park was available for visitors. Adjoining the car park was farmland, rolling away on all sides.

It was a busy lunchtime, with everyone arriving back at the centre and eagerly awaiting their meal. People milled around chatting and children ran, laughing, among the cars. Suddenly, everyone froze in horror. The farmer, having alighted from his tractor and walked a little way from it, was now shouting a warning as the tractor, obviously left in gear, was moving under its own steam and careering towards the busy car park. The incline was sharp and the huge vehicle quickly built up speed, heading towards the crowd and the children. No one could think what to do, and fear rooted people in the path of danger.

However, miraculously, just as the tractor approached the car park, it swung violently to the right, avoiding people and cars by yards, and went hurtling on down the 60-foot cliff. The people on top of the cliff were safe, but the tractor was now speeding down the cliff towards Andrew, who had witnessed all this from the doorway of his chalet. It was certain to career straight into him and this was all happening at such speed that Andrew was at a loss to know which way to run. It was at this point that, yet again only yards from people, the tractor turned sharply to the right, this time turning over and smashing with force into Andrew's car and completely demolishing it. Everyone was astounded at these events; the people from the car park came running down, while several monks who had also witnessed the incident arrived at the scene. The monks and Andrew had seen a figure inside the tractor, pulling the wheel and steering it away from the crowds and Andrew. Yet how could this be, for the farmer had watched in dismay as his empty tractor leaped into action? The monks arrived on the scene first and rushed to the wreckage, desperate to pull free the man they had seen. There was, however, no one in the wreckage, nor anywhere near. The tractor was completely empty. Andrew and all the other witnesses are still completely baffled today, ten years later.

Although many people there felt sure that the figure they had seen was an angel, Andrew was not one of those to leap immediately to this conclusion. However, as he went on to say to me, what other explanation could there be?

Angel rescues are not confined to any particular spot on the globe – their presence is known all over the world. A report of the following episode reached me from Africa. Angel stories have probably always been part of wartime situations, and the First World War has proved to be a particularly rich source of such experience. The Old Testament of the Bible not only has many accounts of wars and battles but also angelic or divine intervention. In one such story, the prophet Elisha sees enemy forces surrounded by another army, although this second army is one which can only be seen when spiritual eyes are open. Whatever other feelings may be evoked by the violent clashes, which are often described so graphically in the Bible, this story clearly has a message about protection, support and care (see 2 Kings 6.8-17) and is mentioned in the following account collected from an Assistant Bishop in Rwanda, a country which has in recent times been subject to the ravages of war and accompanying persecutions. These details are taken from an article in *Yes*, the magazine of the Church Missionary Society, and are used by kind permission. At many different stages Bishop Alexis Bilindabagabo feared not only for his own life and for members of his family, but also for many of his fellow Tutsis. There were several occasions on which he seemed to have remarkable escapes from forces pursuing him, eventually being able to flee to Zaire. The account given in full here is one in which he tells of his belief that angels were responsible for his protection and that of many others. He feels that those who would have attacked were prevented from doing so by angelic forces. He is also very aware that he is now in a position where he must continue to find the ability to go on loving the people of his country, in spite of all the persecution

28

which he has faced. To him, God's peace and protection was not only real for the episode described here and others, but is something for him to take into the future. The following is taken from a CMS Ireland video made by George Pitt.

'All the Tutsis around the diocesan headquarters in Kigeme had been killed, except for those who had managed to escape and were with us in a big multi-purpose hall in a secondary school. It was on a Sunday at around midday. Kigeme is a hilly place and, from the top of the hill where we were, we could see hundreds of people coming, armed with various weapons. They stopped at a distance from us.

'Three people then came to us. I think they were spies, trying to see if we had some weapons, if there was going to be any resistance. They met me in front of the hall where we had three hundred refugees, including my family. We were all gathered together and had been praying. We had been praying for two days and teaching people how to receive Jesus Christ, to repent of their sins and to prepare for heaven.

'So these three people came to me and told me, "Bishop, we come to tell you that people are coming to kill you." I asked if they could give them a message. They laughed – they *pretended* to laugh.

'The words that had come into my mind were from 2 Kings, when Elisha, the servant of God, was surrounded by an army bigger than that of the enemies who were coming to destroy him. I told them, "You go and tell them that this hill is surrounded by many angels. If these angels allow you, then you will come and destroy us. But if they don't allow you, nobody will approach us. So we are ready. Go and tell them that we are ready. We are not afraid."

'We waited. Thirty minutes later, they just stopped a hundred metres short of the hall where we were. We heard the whistles, meaning that the leaders were telling them to go away. We saw them going – and I was aware that it was the angels who had restrained the army which was surrounding this hill.'

We move from Africa to South America for our next story. Many people who have contributed to this book talk about guardian angels, and the belief in guardian angels is certainly widespread. The attraction of the idea that there is 'someone looking after us' is indeed universal. We love to feel that there are figures who have a greater power than us and who can rescue us from danger through this power. At the same time, they are very personal to us in meeting our needs, and this comes out strongly in what Inelia has to say.

Few people will ever need an angel more than Inelia did at the time when her angel protected her in Valparaiso in Chile, more than 20 years ago. It was not a happy time to be living in this part of South America. Inelia was working as a lecturer at the University of Valparaiso and, being socially aware, she was a member of a group working for the underprivileged in society. She had always held left-wing views, serving on the local council, working as hard as she could to ease the harsh life of those less fortunate than herself. This was frowned on by right-wing factions and in the autumn of 1973 great changes were about to overtake her and all her compatriots. The civilian government led by President Allende was about to be ousted in a bloody coup. A military junta led by General Pinochet came to power, a frightening time for anyone holding socialist views. Killings and oppression were the order of the day.

The coup happened on 11 September 1973 and a curfew was immediately imposed on the population. People were allowed outdoors for only two hours during daylight, and after dark you took your life in your own hands if you ventured out. It was against this backdrop of fear that Inelia had to make a very important decision: whether or not to try to attend her left-wing group meeting.

'We had been unable to communicate and I was becoming increasingly worried about the fate of my colleagues. I felt I had to find out if they were safe and what, if any, were their plans. All our lives were in jeopardy from the military, and so it was with great anxiety that I planned to visit the meeting arranged before the events of 11 September.

'There was no public transport and private transport was forbidden, leaving only one option, a half hour's walk through dark, dangerous streets. Military patrols marched on foot and patrolled in lorries carrying machine guns, and would shoot the minute they saw anyone outdoors. Knowing all this, and being terribly afraid, I still felt compelled to go and find my comrades.

'I dressed in the darkest clothing I possessed, a long, dark brown coat and boots. I wound a dark brown scarf around my head. I am short of stature, being less than five feet tall, and I thought this, along with my dark clothing, might help me to melt into the shadows.

'It was extremely dark as I set out, my heart pounding and my legs shaking, walking as close as possible to the wall and trying not to make a sound. The patrols were not the only fear I had; I was also acutely aware of the danger I faced from dogs. Everyone, it seemed, kept a dog, not a cute, friendly pet but working dogs – large, ferocious guard-dogs which patrolled the gardens of most houses. I had to work out how to pass the houses on my route without disturbing the dogs. With great trepidation I reached the large house with a small fence bordering a very long and large garden. It was totally dark, but at the very end of the garden I could make out two enormous shapes. My mouth went dry as I stood, transfixed, trying to decide what to do.

'The decision was suddenly made very much harder by the sound of foot patrols coming in my direction and I was so terrified I could scarcely breathe. I had a choice between being mowed down by machine guns or attacked by fierce, huge dogs. In an instant I decided to make for a clump of bushes just inside the gate and I plunged into them as the soldiers came around the corner and the two dogs, barking and snarling, came hurtling down the garden towards me.

'The terror of that moment will live with me for ever. I thought my last minutes had arrived, and realised that there was nothing I could do but pray.

'Ever since I was a very small girl, my mother had taught me to pray and talk to my guardian angel. "Your angel is always watching over you," she taught me, "and in times of need, you must ask for help." I would never need my angel more. I closed my eyes and asked for help fervently.

'The noise of the dogs increased, but I felt them run straight past me to the fence, where they barked ferociously at the soldiers. The soldiers would have had little compunction in shooting the dogs had they been able to be sure that it was they who had caused them to bark. However, in their uncertainty they decided to move on and leave the dogs to guard the grounds. At that point I dared to open my eyes, only to see that the dogs had spotted me and were coming racing towards me once more. I called on my angel again, and this time I felt such a presence, such a powerful feeling of love and protection. The dogs bounded up to me and merely sat one on either side in silence, and even licked my face! I could feel the presence all around, calming the dogs, calming me. I saw no bright, shining angel or even light, but I felt the presence as strong and supportive as a rock.

'Finally composing myself, I continued on to the meeting, eventually arriving very late, but finding, to my horror, no one there, and knowing instinctively that they had been discovered. So my angel had saved me from the soldiers, the dogs and discovery that night.

'Difficult times followed, but I have never forgotten that incident, nor my angel who protects me still to this very day.'

Inelia had never told her story in its entirety before, and was most insistent that it be recorded and published. Sadly, only weeks after relating her story she died suddenly from a heart attack. This testimony of her courage is now revealed as she wished – a fitting memorial.

Further proof, if any were needed, of the global network of angels in action comes from Australia, a short but thought-provoking account from a schoolgirl who had very timely help indeed from her angel. It happened in Perth, Western Australia, and although Elizabeth is now an adult, her school adventure is as clear in her mind now as it was that hot sunny day.

She was a pupil at a girls' school, noted for its high academic standards and with an excellent sporting record. A firm favourite when it came to leisure pursuits was horse-riding. The school was set in extensive grounds and beyond them were vast areas of bushland with very little in the way of civilisation. From time to time, a whole day's riding would be organised, and many students would look forward to this.

It was on one of these day trips that Elizabeth found herself riding next to a new girl, fresh from England. It seemed to be a bit of harmless fun to tease her about the dangers of the bush, and for some time this became an amusing pastime for Elizabeth.

At one point in the trek, they came across a shallow-looking river, and the teachers rounded up horses and riders to cross in single file. They positioned themselves mid-stream, to see all the students safely to the opposite bank. Elizabeth and the new girl were right at the end of the line, and for a joke Elizabeth told the by now distinctly nervous girl to watch out for crocodiles as they always took the last person crossing! The poor girl was terrified, not knowing how rare it was for crocodiles to be spotted at this particular point. They slowly made their way to the opposite bank, the new girl white-faced and trembling. Emerging on to dry land, the teacher asked her if she was alright. She said that she was, but that the crocodile had nearly caught her – had she not asked her guardian angel to protect her, she was certain she would have been attacked. The other girls laughed loudly, aware of the dozens of times they'd crossed that particular river and knowing that a crocodile in these parts was as rare as snow. The teacher smiled and said, 'You probably saw a dead tree branch. No one can ever remember seeing a crocodile here.' The girl looked relieved. She turned her horse around to look back across the river, and there, to everyone's consternation, lying in the shallows was a huge crocodile. Riding away with all the speed they could manage, they arrived back at school, shaken and red-faced. Perhaps in the future they would be more inclined to take both crocodiles and angels seriously.

Angels helping in battles or guarding us from dangerous animals are very dramatic forms of rescue, but it seems that they may also save us from circumstances or when we are in a tight corner, not knowing where to turn next. Sharif's story is one such account, an incident which stands out in an already eventful life, in which he has experienced more than a little hardship. His meeting with what he is sure is his guardian angel perhaps reflects some of the changes which have happened in more recent years for him, and it also reminds us that angels do not always need to appear with wings.

Sharif endured a very unhappy English childhood. Violence was an everyday occurrence and he grew up with much unhappiness and many problems. Eventually, he became involved in a shady world of crime and drugs, which did not stop him continuing to experience overwhelming feelings of despair. He was living on the streets, without a job or qualifications to find one, and he was forced into crime in order to survive. Sinking lower and lower in a spiral of self-loathing, he contemplated suicide – it seemed to be the only way out.

At this low point, one night a set of circumstances made him stumble across a group of people about to attend a prayer meeting. He was invited into the house with them, and they offered him fellowship and gave him a sense of acceptance. With their help he started back on the road to normality. It was a long and hard one, and it took years to overcome the pain and the long history of loneliness. Eventually, however, the healing process was complete. Sharif had been brought up as a Moslem but now decided to become a Christian. He attended Bible college and became involved with youth and community work. He felt restored and happy, even though life was still a struggle, with just enough money for basic needs.

Hearing of an international Christian meeting in Germany, Sharif was determined to go, despite his financial difficulties. Armed with virtually no money and carrying only a small rucksack, he set off for a Channel port, hitching rides to enable him to buy his ferry ticket. Sailing across the English Channel, however, he realised with sinking heart that he was at a loss as to what he might do next. Having very little money left, he knew that on disembarking from the ferry he had a problem. Firstly, he had to get to Frankfurt. Hitchhiking in Germany is illegal, so he could not rely on friendly motorists. However, on leaving the boat and slinging the rucksack on his shoulder he felt a weight which had not been there before. Investigating, he discovered that the bottom of the rucksack was filled with twenty-pence pieces! Totally astonished and completely bewildered as to where they had come from, he started to count them. When he had completed the task he exchanged them for deutschmarks and found he had 96. He ran to the train station and enquired about a ticket to Frankfurt. He was told the cost was 96 deutschmarks! There can seldom have been a train ticket purchased with greater joy and soon he was on his way to Frankfurt.

It was late that night and pitch black when the train arrived at Frankfurt, the joy of arriving quickly evaporating when Sharif realised that his problems were still pretty acute. Wiesbaden was his eventual destination and he still had no money. What then were the options? Should he sleep on a bench in the park and see what the morning brought? Or should he start to walk? No, it was obviously much too far. Confused, he stood on the platform at 3 a.m., feeling increasingly anxious. A young couple appeared on the deserted platform and to his relief they spoke English. They listened to his dilemma and agreed to find the stationmaster to see if he might be able to help. They climbed the stairs and crossed the long bridge linking the platform on which Sharif stood with the opposite platform and the stationmaster's office. Sharif, alone again, did the only thing he could in these circumstances. He prayed silently, asking God and his angels to help him. He saw the stationmaster talking to the young couple. Then, at this point, as if by magic, a second man appeared. It was hard to see where he had come from. The station-master's office door was closed and had he walked across the bridge Sharif would have seen him. At this moment, the young people shouted and waved, telling him not to worry because everything was in hand.

Bewildered, Sharif saw the stationmaster talk to the second man. This man was wearing a bright red cap and Sharif assumed that he was some higher-ranking rail-way official. The station was still deserted and Sharif watched as the stationmaster walked across the bridge and down on to the platform on which Sharif stood. This took several minutes, during which time Sharif looked across at the man in the red cap, but, to his amazement, he seemed to vanish before his eyes and appear on Sharif's platform ahead of the stationmaster. The stationmaster came up to Sharif and said in broken English to Sharif's surprise, 'Travel arrangements have already been made for you. You have a seat booked on the next train at 4 a.m. The ticket is already paid for in your name.' Sharif could scarcely believe his ears. He span around to find the man in the red cap had again disappeared.

The train arrived and, silently thanking God, he climbed aboard, noticing that on the far platform stood, yet again, the mysterious figure in the red cap, staring across the train tracks at Sharif. Sitting down, Sharif puzzled how on earth this man could move from one platform to the other without crossing the bridge, and in seconds. He pulled down the window and popped his head out as the train started to move. Sure enough the man appeared in front of him. This time Sharif saw his face clearly, shining and radiant, with piercing blue eyes and a halo of light surrounding him. Sharif knew at once that this was his guardian angel, sent from God to help him.

M any people have found themselves in difficulty while swimming. Straying too far out or getting out of one's depth are common occurrences, but most people struggle back to shore or are rescued by lifeboat or life-guard. Not everyone is as lucky, however, as Mary discovered.

'I believed myself to be a strong swimmer and therefore was perhaps less careful than most in the sea. I worked as a nurse and needed a full-time hobby which would be relaxing and refreshing, in order to combat the stress of my job, and swimming seemed ideal. With this in mind, I was looking forward to a holiday on which I could swim daily if I so desired. A group of friends had asked me to join them on a trip to Gibraltar and we all set off in high spirits. The holiday was all I had hoped it would be – relaxing, lots of sunshine, good company and a lovely beach.

'One day, at the end of a hot afternoon, I decided to

have a long, leisurely swim before returning to the hotel for the evening. Most people were gathering their belongings and leaving the beach. No one else was swimming. Striking out from the shore, I felt strong and calm, enjoying the late sun on my back, and thinking only how pleasant this all was. I was far too relaxed, because when I eventually stopped swimming and looked back, I realised just how far out I had gone. The beach was on the distant horizon and the sun was going down; the sea was becoming choppy.

'I realised just how tired I was and thought despairingly of the distance I must cover to reach the shore. No matter how hard I tried to swim back, I made very little progress, the swell hampering me at every stroke. Panic was rising inside me, and then I resigned myself to what I believed to be the inevitable – I was to die here. This must be my destiny, so I tried to float and absorb this latest fact, alone in what appeared to be a vast stretch of water.

'Suddenly, in front of me appeared the face of an elderly gentleman. I was too surprised and weak to say anything, but he smiled and placed a firm hand beneath my chin, pulled me after him, and struck out for the shore in the traditional rescue stroke. The distance was enormous, but we were on the beach in what felt like seconds. It was wonderful to feel the beach beneath my feet as I was gently pulled from the shallows.

'I sat coughing, the firm but gentle hands on my shoulders. The beach was deserted, as was the bay, not a boat or a swimmer in sight. How lucky I'd been, saved from certain drowning. I felt the hands leave my shoulders, and I turned to thank my rescuer – only to find no one there. I was completely alone on the beach! I realised instantly that the rescue, the feelings of security and warm love, were all due to my guardian angel.

'Many times since, in moments of need or anxiety, I have felt again those wonderfully reassuring hands on my shoulders.'

Most people, as Mary did, feel relief, peace and gratitude flowing through them when in contact with angels. Sometimes, however, the feelings are initially of pure fright. Ann, an American woman who lives in Yorkshire, England, tells a unique story. She was shown what seemed almost like a 'video' of what might happen if she did not intervene.

'It was Christmas Eve 1978. I was 15 and lived in Overland Park, Kansas. Nothing extraordinary ever had occurred around this time, and I was not on any medication that would induce hallucinations. I had never seen any "paranormal presence" before (or since). I was asleep in my bed and my poodle was curled up beside me as usual. As I slept, I had the sensation of someone picking up my right wrist and shaking it firmly. I remember thinking that it was unlike the way that anyone in my family would wake me up. At first I ignored it, and I think, as I involuntarily became more awake, I even uttered the words, "Go away!" (as any reasonable teenager would). It did not go away and I remember crossly opening one eye to see who had hold of my wrist. But I could see no one. This was strange. Then I noticed that my dog, who had been curled up by my side, had stirred and was now standing at full attention, facing the foot of my bed. She never barked or shivered, but simply stood at attention.

'It was at this point that I came fully awake, because I now realised that something unusual was taking place and that I needed to be alert. I was scared. I knew that I should look at the foot of my bed, but I couldn't bring myself to do so. I was aware of an unnatural light (I could see my bedroom clearly, although it was dark in the hallway outside my room) and of a "presence", like the feeling you get when you know that someone is staring at you, even though your back is to them.

'It was then that I heard a voice saying, "It's OK, I won't hurt you". I heard it a few more times before I trusted it enough to turn and look. Slowly, I turned my head and saw with my physical eyes a huge woman at the foot of my bed. She was silent, smiling benevolently, as I took a good look at her. She was taller than the height of my room, as if my ceiling did not exist where she stood, and yet I could clearly see the ceiling below her head height in other areas of the room. She was also stocky and wore her hair in an old-fashioned bun style. Her dress was long and purple. The most striking feature for me at this time was the light that was radiating around her. I could see through her, and yet she seemed solid to me. But the light . . . I could feel it on my body, warm and lovely!

'Did I enjoy this wonderful experience? I was terrified! At the same time, I somehow knew that I was safe and was aware of the peace I felt with her. I wasn't frightened of her, but I was frightened that I was insane. I addressed her for the first time, "Who are you?"

'She answered (although no audible words were spoken), "You can call me Judith." I don't know why, but I asked, "Are you my guardian angel?" She smiled more widely than ever and said, almost with a laugh, "You could say that . . ." She then told me that I was to watch carefully, because she was going to show me something. I watched obediently, as she showed me a scene of my great-grandmother getting up to make breakfast in her own kitchen in Florida. I saw my great-grandmother put a slice of toast in the toaster, and as she pressed the lever down, the toaster sparked and she fell dead to the floor. I then saw a tombstone with her name on it and the date read 27 December 1978, just three days away.

'My obedience dissolved into an intellectual and emotional struggle. Why had I been shown this? I convinced myself that I was definitely insane and started to work out what to do about it. I thought about all the options and I decided that I would have to tell someone, because the earlier I started treatment, the sooner

I would be well again. I somehow decided that if I worked really hard, I would probably be released from psychiatric hospital in three years' time and then I could resume my schooling. It sounds absurd, I know, but is absolutely true.

'I don't know how long I spent sitting in bed working out my bid for sanity, but I became increasingly aware of Judith trying to break through. The same scene was played again, but this time she told me, "Tell your mother; she will know what to do." The scene and this message were repeated as if it were a loop recording, finally exhausting me into submission. It gave me hope that she was offering me a course of action, but then I began worrying that my mother would think I was insane. Judith tried to comfort me with her light. My body was calm and peaceful, it was my mind that couldn't be comforted. The scene stopped being played, and I saw only Judith again. She kept saying, "Tell your mother." She then left in an instant, and I was very aware of the darkness around me.

'I didn't sleep after that. I lay in bed and knew that I had to tell my mother. I was still frightened about what had happened. I got out of bed on Christmas morning, long after I had heard excited and happy voices coming from downstairs. I decided to get it over with. My mother came out of her room at the same time that I came down the hallway towards the room. My mother recalls that I was ashen-white. "I can't go downstairs," I said to her. "I can't have Christmas. Grandma Taylor is going to die." "What do you mean?" said my mother. "You'll think I'm crazy. There was an angel in my bedroom last night," I said.

'My mother was shocked at this, but something told her to take it seriously. I then told her about the events of the night in detail, including what I had been shown. She was rather taken aback that I should have been shown something as traumatic as the sudden death of my great-grandmother, but then began to wonder to what extent this was a warning and things could be changed. I then stressed what Judith had told me about telling my mother, saying she would know what to do. All that she could think of doing was to telephone her own mother, who was Grandma Taylor's daughter.

'I was still worried about my experience but my mother comforted me, saying that some people do see angels. I was so relieved that she hadn't laughed, scolded or disbelieved me. Now that I knew someone was prepared to believe me (and didn't think I was mad) I had a feeling of absolute trust in the reality and genuineness of what had happened. My mother went ahead and telephoned her own mother to tell her what had happened. As my grandmother also lived in Florida, she was in the habit of keeping a regular check on her parents.

'My mother was not completely without concern as to how my grandmother would react on hearing the story. However, at the part when she mentioned the toaster, the reaction was, "Oh my God! That toaster scares me to death!" My grandmother explained that the toaster her parents owned was very old and quite often sparked and made spluttering noises. In order to save money my great-grandfather would take it into the garage and try and fix it rather than buy a new one. She also said that when her mother had recently visited the doctor he had been concerned about her and had gone as far as telling the rest of the family that her heart was so bad that she should not get angry, excited or frightened. One interesting aspect of their discussion was that the description of the toaster I had seen matched exactly the offending article, which was of a particularly unusual design.

'My mother and grandmother decided that the toaster should be removed immediately. My mother asked if there was anywhere that my grandmother could buy a replacement straightaway as a Christmas present, hardly likely on Christmas Day, but my grandmother exclaimed, "I forgot! I've got a brand new one in the garage still in its box. I'll take care of it." And she did.

'My great-grandmother died in October 1980, having enjoyed a further two years of life.'

We have seen various incredible forms of rescue. The following story is an example of intervention coming mainly through voices rather than vision or sensation. It is nonetheless a rescue from a desperate situation. Out of inner turmoil came a gentle stilling of the soul and a firm guiding hand back on to an even path. I have left Pam's story as she recounted it.

'It is now nearly ten years since I had an experience which changed my life completely from the moment it happened and which I remember vividly in every detail to this day. It took place in a remote river valley in Wales. My former husband and I had a little holiday cottage there, which was situated on the hillside, 900 feet above the river, with breathtaking views across the hills, a waterfall cascading down by the side of the woodland which bordered our property; no telephone, no TV or radio, nothing but peace and the sound of birds and the river below. We first went there for holidays with the family, but as the children grew up, more for the respite it gave us from jobs and the weekly grind. Then we began to go up there singly, and I started to use it on my own at weekends to try and "sort myself out", as I was becoming increasingly unhappy. Usually, the cottage performed its "magic". I would go up there on Friday nights, drink in the solitude, feeling all the tension physically drain away, but also fighting the fear of the first night alone there in the black isolation.

'On that particular Sunday afternoon in the autumn, I had packed the car up and closed the cottage down, but I just could not leave. I had arrived on Friday in a very depressed state, and I was not ready to make the journey home. At about 4 p.m., with the car and cottage locked up, I set out once more on my favourite walk along the river valley, hoping to be in an easier frame of mind by the time I went home. My thoughts were still jangling inside my head as I walked, or rather strode along, because I knew I had to be on my way before it got really dark. The noise in my head was almost deafening, when, above it all, I heard a shout, "Listen to me!" I stopped and quickly turned round, suddenly aware that I was very much on my own and that it was getting dark. It came again, almost wearily, but very plainly; "Please, please, listen to me."

'I had stopped dead in my tracks in the middle of the lane. All the agitation completely left me. I remember my mind going blank, and then I walked very slowly over to a field-gate by the side of the lane, resting my arms on it and listening. I was listening to the most beautiful words that I had ever heard in my life. I cannot remember the content, but as the voice went on, I began to feel warm and comforted, as if I was being enfolded in someone's arms. As I listened, thoughts and images were coming of a very different life, one of love and harmony. A deep knowledge and understanding began to form in my mind. There was going to be a way to find the peace and love and contentment I so desperately needed, and I was always going to have help. From now on I did not have to struggle on my own, because somebody would always be there. But, true to form, I had to question this. I remember asking out loud, "How will I find you? How will I know you? I don't go to church."

'The lovely voice said, "The whole world is my church. Wherever you are you can reach me. Look up! You are standing in one of my cathedrals now."

'I looked up and the crags and cliffs of that valley almost met over my head like a vaulted roof. When I lowered my eyes again, everything slipped into perspective, and I was looking at the field, conscious of the gate I was leaning on. How long I had been there I will never know, whether it was seconds, minutes, or longer.

I looked around the meadow and up at the cliffs, which seemed very ordinary now, but I felt a completely different person. I walked calmly back to the cottage, got into the car and drove home. I had an inner peace that I had never experienced before. I felt a strength and ease of mind, which was totally new, and this was only the beginning. All my frantic agitation and hopelessness went that afternoon and has never returned.

'In the following months, in spite of what my Friend had said, I went to church to renew my faith and find the support to reshape my life. Soon afterwards, Roy, who is now my husband, but had been my first boyfriend of 30 years ago, walked back into my life, and since then new doors have opened. We have a wonderful life, with so much love and happiness through friends and family. So much of everything. Both of us know the very real presence of our Friend. We trust his being completely.

'I had not spoken of this experience in any detail to anyone except my father, who had a strong Christian belief, and more superficially to my daughters, who raised their eyebrows, until I attended a workshop on angels a few months ago. Only then, in the company of others who had similar spiritual experiences, did I realise that my Friend is indeed a guardian, a guardian angel.

'At no time was this more evident than when my father died. I had been at the nursing home all day with my father, who had been very ill for some time. We had been told to come as the doctor had finally started to administer morphine. It was a long and difficult day for my father. I said many prayers that day, and eventually he died, while I was away for an hour. I was devastated at not being there for the final moments with him. After I had seen the doctor and rung everyone in the family with the news, I said I was ready to go home, a journey of 60 miles.

'As I got into the car, completely numb, I remember thinking that I hoped the police would be understanding if I went through a red light or round a roundabout the wrong way, but there were no problems. My hands never left the steering wheel in the whole of that 60-mile drive. All I had was the black road in front of me. I never saw another car. It was as if the road ahead had been swept clean of all traffic and every light set at green.

'When I arrived home and Roy saw the state I was

in, he asked me how on earth I had driven home. I said that I had not driven home, I had been brought home! Indeed, I know that my Friend will always "bring me home".'

Bringers of Comfort

Light and life to all he brings,
Risen with healing in his wings
CHARLES WESLEY

We can see from the rescue stories that angels are still helping people in our own times, and have great impact on the individuals who experience them, often changing their lives completely. Each of these events, although very personal, reminds us of the involvement of angels with humanity as a whole. This involvement goes back thousands of years and can be found in the literature and mythology of many cultures. There is much evidence of their presence not just within individuals but with larger groups.

Angels are indeed figures of mercy, and people with a strong desire to help others are referred to as 'angels'. Florence Nightingale was a prime example of this, working with soldiers in the Crimean War. Passing along the rows of beds at night with her lantern, she was often literally believed to be an angel by some badly injured men.

It is no surprise, then, that many stories include angels healing and helping in times of illness, and when people have a brush with death. The first account in this section is vivid and moving and must surely have been an experience which George would have remembered for the rest of his life, after it had happened.

Several years ago, my father worked for a large international company of haulage contractors, which employed many drivers for their huge fleet of lorries. My father's job was to map out the routes, work out timetables, and to pay the wages each weekend.

George was the leader of this group of men. Having grown up in a large and very poor family in an area of Liverpool, England, where survival was a struggle, he had learned to fight for his rights, for his own protection and that of his younger brothers and sisters. He had a reputation for being a 'hard man', and his enormous height and bulk meant that George was not to be messed with. Many times he waded in and separated men fighting, nor was he beyond starting a fight himself. Colourful language and heavily tattooed arms completed the picture of a man one would not like to cross.

One day, George was visiting the office to collect his wages and almost shyly asked my father if he would do him a favour to be carried out in complete secrecy, as confidentiality was of the utmost importance in this matter. My father said that he would help if at all possible and promised faithfully not to say a word to the other drivers. It transpired that George had a terrible toothache but was terrified of visiting the dentist. He had, however, made an appointment and knew that one or more teeth would need to be removed, so he wanted my father to go with him.

The day arrived and my father collected George in his car. He was shocked to see him white-faced and trembling. George's worst fears were confirmed at the surgery, as several teeth needed to be removed straightaway to stop the pain he was in. When the extractions were completed, the dentist started to revive George from the anaesthetic, but to his horror found that he could not do so, since he had been given too much. Frantically the dentist worked on him while his assistant called the doctor, who arrived almost instantly. Although George had indeed 'died', the doctor managed to restart his heart and revive him. It took a long time before he was well enough to travel home.

Home again and feeling much better, he sipped a cup of tea and started chatting to my father about what he had experienced while under the anaesthetic. He had had a classic near-death experience, travelling swiftly down a long dark tunnel, emerging into a bright light that emanated peace and calm. He felt wonderfully content, but a voice told him that he must go back as it was not yet time for his life on earth to end. He then found himself hurtling with great speed back into his own body. On regaining consciousness he opened his eyes and saw the dentist and doctor, but standing behind them was a large angel, wings outstretched with a look of caring and love on its face. He felt a strong sensation of well-being and the knowledge that he would be cured. My father, a religious man, listened to all this with great interest and they talked for hours about the whole episode.

George insisted that no one should ever know of this for fear of ridicule, and his story remained a secret until my father related it to me after George died. I don't think George would mind his story being told today, for his angel was very special.

Angels care for us in times of stress and great need, in much the same way as parents. They often intervene, it seems, when all else fails.

Millie had arrived at such a point. Her story is a life-saving and life-restoring one. She is now a happy, normal 22-year-old student, thoroughly enjoying her university course, friends and family, and looking forward to the future. However, only two years ago the future looked very black indeed and she was in despair.

'I had been suffering from depression for four years. I felt very low indeed and had arrived at a point where I was so ill and depressed that I knew I was close to death. I was taking medication, but strongly believe that the drugs concerned were not the cause of the following incident, which is similar to many other near-death experiences.

'I had the sensation of flying at great speed through

56

a long dark tunnel, at the end of which a figure was waiting to receive me. I could not tell its gender, but it was tall and clothed in a long white cloak. As I approached, it extended a hand towards me in welcome. I knew instinctively that if I took the hand proffered I should be entering heaven. Despite feeling dreadfully ill and depressed I did not want my life to end and I asked if I might continue to live.

'I was allowed to return and was filled with great elation and hope. In hospital during my slow recovery I saw angels on several occasions in the form of cherubs. One incident was especially awe-inspiring: cherubs appeared accompanied by a central figure whom I felt to be a deity. Was it really God? Certainly its appearance was very much how my imagination had always seen God – a smiling, loving, friendly, bearded figure.

'These events took place when I felt beyond help of any other kind: family, friends, my G.P., the hospital with all its scientific resources. I was at last feeling better and more secure; hope returned, and I knew that I would live and that my future would be happy and fulfilling. Since that time I have not seen any angels, but I know that they are real, that they are here to help and that I am never alone.'

Many people have told me in their accounts that they know they were dying and were then spared, for different reasons. This was certainly the case for Lilian: she was certain that the responsibility of looking after two small children played a central role in her restored health. This is a story from northern England, Bolton, in the heart of Lancashire. Lilian subsequently related it to her two daughters, one of whom has given me this account.

At the time that this incident took place, Lilian's daughters were quite young. Life was a struggle for her physically due to a disabling chest condition. That winter, Lilian was to experience her worst ever illness, so close to death that there was little that could be done to help her. She was at her lowest ebb as she lay in bed, terribly weak.

Suddenly there appeared not one but four magnificent angels, surrounded by light and ready to accompany her on the journey to the next life. She felt herself lifted and carried down a dark tunnel with light at the end, feeling peaceful and free from pain. Then a voice said, 'You must go back. This is not the right time. You have two little girls to take care of.' Her next recollection was being back in bed as the four angels gradually faded away, leaving her to start a slow recovery – much to her surprise and that of those who were close to her. Lilian died many years later, but not before she had been able to tell her daughters of her amazing experience.

Not all angel experiences are dramatic. Sometimes, although a figure and a light may appear, the feelings are soft and gentle. The situation may not be a life-threatening one, but perhaps an occasion where support is greatly needed. Kate was in just such a situation, released from hospital and rather nervous to be alone, but reassurance and help was close, as she tells us.

'I was keen to leave hospital after an operation – perhaps too keen for my own good – but I felt secure in the knowledge that my husband would be collecting and looking after me. However, on leaving the hospital, he told me that owing to business circumstances he would have to leave me on my own. He was most distressed, but I assured him, with a confidence I did not feel, that I would be fine. Settling me on a sofa, with flasks of drinks and sandwiches, he reluctantly left and I lay there feeling weak and very vulnerable. Suddenly, out of the corner of my eye, I saw a light appear and grow in brightness and size, until it assumed the shape of a figure. Such a strong feeling of peace and warmth spread and engulfed me in a sensation of pure love. As the light-figure faded, I fell into a deep sleep and on waking felt revived, healed, and at peace. My recovery was swift and sure, and the belief in my angel unshakeable.'

Gentle intervention is a theme in many of the stories in this book. One could ask, however, why angels do not always rush to help. Perhaps they do, but for various reasons we do not respond or recognise their intervention. Imagine a common scene: someone leaving for a holiday and about to drive away, but deciding to go back to double-check all their windows and doors. This could prevent a house being broken into. On another occasion, something tells you to be extra careful driving down a narrow suburban road, when suddenly a bouncing ball, closely followed by a child, appears in your path. Could this be an example of subtle angelic intervention? Help may be there all the time, but we may choose to ignore it. For many people, however, the intervention and help is so visible that there is no mistaking it.

Mavis discovered this truth when faced with the prospect of losing her much loved mother. Her grandmother had an old saying, 'Never turn a stranger from your door; they might be an angel in disguise.' Mavis also believed in the concept of a personal guardian angel. Some years ago her mother was seriously ill, and she was nursing her. She also had two small children demanding her time and attention, resulting in a very emotional and stressful period of her life. One day her mother was very much worse, and fading fast. The thought of losing her was unbearable, and she did the only thing left to her – she prayed, intensely and desperately, for some time. Suddenly, she was aware of a presence in the room. She opened her eyes and saw two enormous wings of light, the size of the room, filling her vision. Peace, love and healing flowed from them, and she was overwhelmed with a sensation of help and support. Gradually they faded. She stood transfixed, looking down at her mother as a lovely smile spread across her face. She opened her eyes and asked, 'Do you know, I think I'm going to be alright now?' And indeed she was . . .

The next story is very personal for it features my father William. I was, however, astonished to read another very similar account. Both stories feature a visit to a shrine. Angelic presence must be very powerful in such places, owing to the constant flow of prayers. When my daughters were small, we were fortunate enough to be offered the use of a friend's house in Cambridge while they were abroad on holiday. The pleasure of a two-week break was mingled with worry and guilt at leaving my father, who lived alone and suffered from crippling arthritis. However, since he was well cared for by nurses and neighbours, he urged us to go.

Making my usual call to my father one morning before setting out for the day, I was upset to find he had not slept due to severe pain. He could scarcely walk and even though a nurse was with him, I felt sick with worry. I set out for the day with a very heavy heart. After returning from the coast later in the day, we suddenly came upon Walsingham Priory. We went inside the beautiful shrine, where a service was about to begin. The nuns asked if there was anyone we should especially like to pray for. Usually there was a list of names, but that afternoon it was blank. I explained my father's predicament, and one of the nuns said they would centre their service and prayers around him. Taking the girls by the hand, she led them to the altar, and told them to light a candle for Grandpa. They were to ask the angels to help him. This they did, and a lovely short service followed, calming me somewhat.

A couple of hours later we arrived back at the house in Cambridge, and the first thing I did was to ring my father. I was amazed to hear his voice, full of delight and astonishment. 'You'll never guess what happened today,' he said. 'Suddenly this afternoon, all my pain disappeared. I've been able to walk without my sticks and, miraculously, I've climbed the stairs for the first time in two years. Can you believe that?' Stunned and in tears, I told him about Walsingham, and he too cried for joy. I would like to report that he was completely cured, but it was not so. Slowly over the next few days the pain returned, but neither of us ever completely lost our wonder at the day the angels answered our prayers.

Knock is a well-known Catholic shrine in Ireland, and I am sure there must be hundreds of stories directly and indirectly linked to visits there. The following account reached me as I sat thinking about my visit to Walsingham, and it seems appropriate to have these two stories next to each other: two shrines and two families linked by angels. This story, however, differs from the Walsingham story and every other story in this book in one special aspect: Sarah heard angelic music. There are many instances of such music, but this is the only one I have come across in researching this book.

Sarah had lived in the same Belfast suburb all her life. The area had changed of course, but several families were still living close by who had been part of her childhood. She had been accident-prone as a child, and had broken several bones. Now she lay in bed wondering if her recent predicament had some connection with these childhood incidents. A fall on an icy pavement while visiting a friend for tea had resulted in a broken pelvis, a stay of several weeks in hospital and a continued degree of pain even when she returned home. The weeks passed and the pain still seemed constant; walking was a huge effort and Sarah became quite depressed. She knew she must try to walk but it hurt dreadfully and she began to give up the battle.

One afternoon, feeling terribly low, she lay in bed and began to cry softly. Gradually, though, she became aware of a large circle of light at the foot of the bed. The room was already sunny and she could not work out where the brightness was coming from. The light increased in intensity, but did not hurt her eyes, and slowly a figure emerged at the centre. Sarah could not make out its features but saw a 'white silhouette', even brighter than the surrounding light. She felt no fear, only warmth and peace. She also heard a faint, beautiful, very gentle music, and she felt her spirits soar. The figure and the light remained for only a few moments, but Sarah felt uplifted and revitalised. On getting out of bed she discovered that there was no pain and that she could walk with ease. She cried for joy and said a prayer of thanksgiving.

Later that evening, her daughter called and Sarah excitedly related the story to her. To her surprise there was silence at the other end of the line. Finally her daughter asked in a choked voice, 'What time was this, Mum?' She answered, 'Around 2 o'clock, I think.' To her amazement her daughter then told her that at this exact time she and her family had been at Knock, Ireland's best-known shrine, where they had lit candles and prayed for her recovery. Sarah feels that their prayers were heard and answered, and is certain that she was sent a healing angel that summer afternoon.

Angels can make their presence felt through various subtle messages and sensations with no apparent source. As well as music, they can also communicate through fragrance.

You may be familiar with the *Angel Cards* published by Findhorn, the spiritual community in Scotland. The cards contain a picture of an angel with an interpretation. The method is to choose a card at random when needing guidance or help. They are not widely used and would be found in very few households.

One night Andrew was walking home late from the underground station. It was dark, drizzling and windy, so he had his collar turned up. He was not taking much notice of his surroundings, intent on reaching the warmth and comfort of home. He had almost arrived when he saw something at his feet glistening in the street light. It was a small white card which he picked up and discovered it to be an angel card. Andrew had visited Findhorn and was familiar with the cards, but was amazed to find one lying on a London street. He took it home and eventually forgot about it.

Months passed, until another evening when Andrew once again came out of the station and began to walk home. It was early spring and quite cold, and the road was busy with evening traffic as Andrew set off down the hill. He was suddenly aware of a wonderful perfume, quite unlike any he knew, and he was perplexed as to its origin, since there were no flowers to be seen and the perfume was stronger than flowers. Then he heard the click of high heels coming behind him, and two women chatting. For a moment he thought it might be their perfume wafting towards him, but soon they turned off and went into a house. However, the fragrance remained.

Reaching the bottom of the hill, Andrew turned into his own street and walked the mile to his door, still accompanied by the exquisite perfume. Just before reaching home he arrived at the spot where he had found the angel card. Hesitating briefly, he recalled the picture of the angel on the card – and to his amazement, the perfume disappeared.

There did not appear to be any immediate reason for this subtle contact, but time has revealed that there was indeed a message for Andrew, one that has led him into areas he would never have dreamed of going.

Science has yet to produce an 'angelometer' for detecting and measuring angel presence. This is unlikely to happen, but neither has it produced a machine for measuring love, yet no one doubts its existence. We have an in-built sensor that enables us to be aware of love's existence and to know that it is as important to humans as all the things that make up our physical needs. Pure love lacks any selfish motive and has inspired hearts and minds through the ages. Jean's love for her son shines through her wonderful story which begins 20 years ago.

'It had been an ordinary day, looking after my family and retiring to bed in a peaceful frame of mind. The dramatic events which followed are as clear to me now as they were on that December night. I woke suddenly for no apparent reason. Sitting upright in bed I had a strong sense of presence, whose nature I could not even guess. I felt such terror that my throat was dry and I opened my mouth to shout, but no sound emerged. My heart was pounding, breathing was becoming difficult, and a strange tingling gripped me. As I stared into the darkness, a faint form slowly appeared at the foot of the bed. A face gazed upon me, increasing in clarity, with a look of pure love and compassion. I both sensed and saw the figure as a feeling of well-being was radiated towards me. No words were spoken, but I heard the words "fear not", and an accompanying calm came over me. As I gazed upon this face so full of compassion, it slowly started to fade, and the image now before my eyes was of my young son. What could it all mean? Eventually I managed to go back to sleep and related these events the next day to my husband, who was equally puzzled. However, the memory stayed very clear, and I pondered on these events four months later.

'In Easter 1977 my young son was taken ill and admitted to hospital. Our worst fears were realised when tests revealed he was suffering from cancer. It was not treatable, and the prognosis was grim. The illness was terminal, severely invasive cancer of the lymph glands, and he was given three months to live. With virtually no hope, the medical team started the treatment that they would normally give, to try at least to make him more comfortable. The powerful vision of that December night enveloped me and the message "fear not" sustained me. My husband and I are Christians and trust in the Lord. To everyone's astonishment, our son responded to the chemotherapy treatment and recovered completely, defying the prognosis. Today he is 28 years old, physically fit and well, full of life and energy. On many occasions since that time I have had an awareness that he has a guardian angel, and often I am convinced it works overtime to protect him. We are all truly blessed.'

Love for children can be a great inspiration, and the love between partners is also a wonderful bond. When faced with losing that bond, the pain is intense. Helen's story paints a vivid picture of an angelic presence in such a traumatic situation.

'I had known my husband for some time before we married. On paper we were an unlikely match: Peter came from a staunch Roman Catholic background and rarely missed going to mass. I on the other hand grew up in a strongly politically-motivated household where religion was scarcely mentioned.

'However, married life was all we hoped it would be and several years passed harmoniously, Peter attending his church while I was still rather sceptical. Our happiness seemed complete when we realised our first child was on the way. I sailed through a healthy pregnancy, and went into hospital for the birth with great excitement. This excitement was, however, short-lived, for it seemed that everything that could possibly go wrong did so. As time passed the danger to my unborn baby and indeed myself increased. Deterioration was so rapid that I knew I was dying. Unbeknown to me at this time, the consultant, aware of Peter's strong Catholic faith, took him on one side and asked him to whom he should give medical priority – myself or the baby? My poor husband was at his wits' end and asked for a little time to think and compose himself. Minutes were all he had, as he paced the corridor in a frenzy of grief.

'I was slipping in and out of consciousness, with the medical staff fading from view, when suddenly everything went completely black. There was no noise, no light, and no pain. I was lying there in pitch blackness, when a figure slowly emerged, approximately level with the foot of the bed, growing in form and brightness and radiating calmness and love. I asked the figure, "Am I dead?" I felt I must be, but the figure gave me a wonderful smile and answered, "It's not your time. You must go back." The floating feeling of warmth, love and peace made me reluctant. I wanted only to stay in this new, blissful state. The figure I saw had no wings, but I knew it was an angel. A long, pale-blue gown covered its feet and it appeared to hover just above my bed. Slowly it faded, and I became aware once more of the lights of the hospital theatre.

'The following hours and days are a blur, but miraculously my son survived and is now a healthy 15-year-old. Did I dream the angel? Was it the result of hospital drugs? Many would say so, but all I know is that the incident is as clear and fresh in my memory today as on that traumatic night 15 years ago.'

Many people describe their encounter with angels simply in terms of light. They feel their warmth, love and superhuman presence in terms of light, which does not always take on the appearance of a figure yet is described as a 'being'. Margot Grey, a British researcher of near-death experiences (NDEs) describes this light phenomenon as white, blue or golden, often blinding in its brilliance, yet not hurting the eyes. These three colours are common in accounts of angels as well as in NDEs. The appearance of this light is very unlike our normal, earthly experience in that it involves a new kind of 'seeing', which is somehow linked with our feelings. The outer light seems to blend with an inner glow, perhaps our inner angel. It almost always results in long-lasting, positive effects at a deeper level in people's lives, and a continued feeling of love and peace.

One such encounter is told by Janice, who had been in hospital frequently over a period of years. On this occasion, the operation was different.

'I had been told that there was a mortality risk involved in what was to be my last operation, but somehow deep inside I knew I would pull through. At that time I was in a lonely marriage, and I hadn't told my husband about the risk, feeling I couldn't share this with him. The only other person besides myself who knew about it was a very close friend of mine, a nursing sister at another local hospital.

'I was at my lowest point at approximately four o'clock on that March morning, getting over the trauma of having to return to the theatre to have my well worn scar restitched. All the other women in the ward were fast asleep and I was propped on my pillows trying to find a comfortable position. The ward was very peaceful, and I felt as if I was the only occupant of the four-bedded room. A warm glow began to creep over me, and the lighting in the ward began to change. At first I thought it was the sun coming up, but the thick curtains in the ward were closed, and I began to feel that although the light was around my bed, it was also coming from inside me. The sensation was so beautiful, accompanied by such feelings of warmth and safety, that I wanted to cry with happiness. It was as if I were being told that there was someone who under-stood me completely, that my life would change for the better, and from that day it has. I know I was visited by an angel that night, who was also there to help me when I eventually plucked up the courage to leave my husband after 16 years of marriage. I also believe that this angel helped me to find my true soulmate, to whom I am now happily married.'

Many people today are feeling the presence of angels and seeing them, but how many are writing to them? Elizabeth has no doubts about the benefits of this, as her story clearly shows.

'I have always felt the closeness of the angels and their ability to create what I need to fulfil my true desires, although, I must admit, this does not always happen in the way I expect. For this past year I have kept a book of my letters to angels, which is in reality a book of their replies to me. I write the question which comes to my mind, and then immediately write the reply which flows from my pen. Only afterwards do I read the contents, and I am often surprised by what I read. On my birthday, at the exact hour of my birth, I wrote asking for guidance for the coming year. At the time the reply seemed insignificant, but two weeks later I reread it. Only then did I perceive its wisdom.

'A few months ago I was visiting my sister, whose mother-in-law was very near to death, following a third stroke. My sister and her husband were both ill, so I took over the nursing-home visiting. It was only when I sat by the bedside of the very ill, deaf, grim-mouthed lady sleeping before me that I realised just how unprepared I was, so I asked, "OK, angels, what do I do now?"

'As I shut my eyes, I could sense the angels gathering to form a circle around the edges of the room, encircling the bed and me. Others came near the bed, and I simply "knew" what I had to say. Even though the old lady obviously couldn't hear me, I told her that her daughter-in-law was ill, that I had come because I loved her, and that I would continue to come once or twice a day. I felt a little embarrassed saying out loud "We love you", but as I spoke, the expression on her face changed.

'During the next few days, I learned to speak "in my head". No words were spoken aloud, just silent thoughts, and I watched her response. Once, at the silent thought of her dead husband's name, she jerked awake. I "talked" about moving to the light when she was ready, and letting go of her regrets. This was an instance of the response being not entirely what I anticipated: my thought "let go" initiated a request for the commode! When it was time for me to leave her room, the angels took over, surrounding her in healing love. No one knew of the angels' presence; it was my secret. By the end of the week the grim mouth had softened into a half-smile. There were times when she would sit up, talking and eating, and gaining strength by the day. She spoke with a new found, gentle appreciation of the carers in the home.

'Two days after I had returned home, leaving her in the care of the angels, my sister was well enough to resume visiting. The telephone call I received after her first visit was not really a surprise to me. "Guess what I found when visiting today? The old lady's bitterness has changed to gratitude and the room is full of angels."'

4

Angels in our Daily Lives

The Angels keep their ancient places;
Turn but a stone and start a wing!
'Tis ye, 'tis your estranged faces
That miss the many-splendoured thing

FRANCIS THOMPSON

As the last two chapters show, angels are often at our side at times of urgent need and crisis, rescuing us from danger and comforting us in sickness. However, they are also with us throughout the course of our daily lives, even if we are unaware of their presence. Angels have featured in everyday life throughout history, including Biblical times, when they were accepted as part of 'normal life'. They were often messengers or guides, announcing events to people. Long conversations between humans and angels are reported, and often a very ordinary scene would suddenly be transformed by the appearance of angels. An example is the shepherds who were looking after their sheep, when suddenly without warning the angels appeared. No wonder the Bible tells us they were afraid!

Angels often arrive out of the blue, for no apparent reason, but sometimes their message becomes clearer at a later date. These stories are gentler in tone, sometimes even playful. Angels can lighten our lives in more ways than one.

ANGELS OF HEALING

You could not imagine a more mundane setting than a shop in the Corn Exchange in Manchester, England. As the name suggests, this building was once the centre for the buying and selling of corn. It has now been transformed into an interesting selection of shops, stalls and cafes, one of which becomes central to the following story. Hazel, who owns a shop selling crystals and other items, tells this very touching tale.

'I have always seen angels, in fact I used to think that everyone could see them. As a young child, whenever I was alone or sad, I would be surrounded by the most beautiful beings of love and light you can imagine. As I grew older, I began to communicate with the angels more and more until they became my constant source of inspiration and divine love for all beings.

'I have devoted my life to healing myself and others, so it came as no surprise when an angel one day fully manifested in my shop Gaia. What I mean by full manifestation is that the angel was clearly visible to myself and the customers who were present in the shop, as if a real person was standing there. The day had begun much the same way as any other day. It was a Saturday in March 1994. I was busy helping people, when a very fragile and sick-looking man appeared. He was in his late seventies and I was wondering what on earth he was doing in the shop, as he was on a walking frame, and hardly able to stand up. He looked directly into my eyes and said, "I need protection." I asked him from what, and why on earth he was out on his own in such a delicate condition.

'He said that he had come for my help, having read a newspaper article about me several years earlier. He did not know where else to turn and was desperate. He went on to explain that he was being persecuted by a group of young people, who had stolen and then vandalised his mobile invalid carriage. When he had complained to the police, they said they could do nothing to help him as they would have to catch the young people in the act of stealing or vandalising the invalid carriage before they could take any action. The young people also kept breaking into his home to steal his pension, and if he refused to tell them where the money was, they tortured him, burning him with cigarettes and beating him with a leather strap. He then showed me his arms, which were a very unpleasant sight, bruised and burned. Nothing was being done to help him and he had no relatives or friends. I felt very sickened that young people could do this to another person, especially one so old, frail, and totally defenceless.

'I told him I would help him. I chose a beautiful, clear quartz crystal. I said I would dedicate it to his highest good, and to the angels of love, light and divine protection. As I proceeded to do this for him, I turned to face the wall, and became aware of the angels around me. It was the most beautiful energy imaginable, full of wisdom and compassion. As I turned back to face the old man, I saw, clearly visible to myself and all the customers in the shop, an angel. It was about eight feet tall, with blond, curly, shoulder-length hair, shining blue eyes, and a flowing robe of shimmering iridescent light with a sash around its chest. It looked like a waterfall of liquid light. I say "it", for I could not tell if it was male or female. Its beauty was beyond words and even its skin had a translucent golden glow. The angel's wings were folded, which angels can do in a confined space. The angel communicated silently with me, saying it was the archangel Michael and that from now on this old man was under his protection. My prayer had been answered.

'The angel disappeared much as it had arrived, but its energy can still be felt in one corner of the shop. I have decided to tell people about this event, because the angels of light want people to know that they are helping mankind. I believe in angels and see angels every day, but we can all see them if we keep our hearts pure and pray for divine guidance.'

The word 'angel' means messenger, and a recent incident emphasises a message of love. Avril did not see an angel or bright lights, but she feels she received the message very clearly. In the hot summer of 1995 she was feeling very low. Her mother was very ill, and it was clear she was unlikely to recover.

One night, Avril had a clear, powerful dream in which an angel radiated comfort and love. Its face was so bright and the dream so vivid that Avril woke feeling much better. To her surprise, a hymn she had not heard or thought about since early childhood was playing in her head. She found herself singing the hymn 'Guardian angels from heaven so bright'. All the words and the tune came back to her clearly and spontaneously, although it was a memory from so long ago. This puzzled her, but there was a further form of communication which made everything clear.

There arrived in the post from relatives in Australia two lapel pins in the form of angels, one for herself and one for her aunt. It came to Avril immediately that the dream, the hymn and now this sign from Australia were all to tell her that an angel was near and to prepare her for her mother's death. Her despair lifted, and she felt helped and guided and very positive. Instead of something to dread, she began to see her mother's death as a transition to the next life. This enabled Avril to celebrate instead of mourning. Even now she feels a strength from these powerful experiences, and she knows a guardian angel was sent to help her through the darkness into the light.

The following tells the story of how Jo's angel lightened her life.

'My first angel experience was during one of my regular bouts of chemical depression, when the "low" was as low as it could get. Luckily, I have among my friends "angel-aware souls", and suddenly it was as if they had summoned up a beautiful angel for me when I could not. I felt the brush of a wing around my sagging shoulders, a warmth, a breath, a love. At last I felt protected, in a way that I had never experienced before. Coursing through my body at that moment came a white light, seeking out and healing my despair. I was not alone! My fight had gone and so I was left wide open to the experience of the wondrous love of my guardian angel. She is always there in my dark nights, her warmth felt and her love lighting up each corner of the room.

'Angels, bless them, never take no for an answer! How many times have we turned our backs on them, ignoring their outstretched arms, their wisdom and care, giving our own thoughts and actions preference? And what happens? We fall on our faces in a pile of con-fusion and hurt, and promptly ask for their help. What forgiving, patient souls they are, and their humour at our human ways is legendary. Angels stick by us like superglue, but without the loss of skin when we try to extricate them from our egos. How many times have we driven along a quiet lane, only to be 'told' to turn off, stop suddenly or change direction, finding that by doing so we have avoided an accident or a herd of rampant cows, or a tree that crashed down just where we would otherwise have been.'

HELP WITH EVERYDAY PROBLEMS

Sometimes angels have a sense of humour. Dominic's certainly did! I think the humour may also have been directed at a well known British journalist who in December 1995 wrote a sceptical article in the *Radio Times* regarding a television programme about people's angel experiences. She asked ironically if angels had ever found a lost Filofax. Yes, they have!

Dominic was close to panic the morning his Filofax went missing. He was a professional man, whose diary was filled with appointments, and the loss of his Filofax would reduce his week to chaos. He started to think about help from on high. Pondering if he really did believe there were angels and if indeed they would perform such mundane tasks, he found himself saying, 'Well, if you're there and can hear me, please help!'

Shortly after this he recalled visiting the bank earlier that day. It seemed logical to go in and see if he had left his Filofax there. On entering the bank, he saw that all the tellers were very busy, with a long queue. He then noticed a desk with a young woman sitting there and thought she might possibly know if the Filofax had been found. On enquiring, he was delighted to hear her say, 'Yes, we have found it and I'll go and get it for you.' While she was momentarily away, Dominic's eyes alighted on the plate on her desk, bearing her name. He had been talking to Dawn Angel. Strangely, he hasn't seen her in the bank since.

Yet another example of angels helping in everyday tasks happened before the start of an important seminar. The seminar leader was desperate to find the bunch of keys which contained not only his house and car keys, but keys for his office and safe. He resolved to allow angels to come in and calm the anxiety threatening to overwhelm him. He asked for help and then walked into the kitchen to make a cup of tea. He stood drinking it at the only spot in the kitchen from which there was a clear view of the refrigerator top – on which lay the keys, normally the last place he would have looked.

ANGELS WHO WARN AND PROTECT

Those who are old enough to remember the 1960s clearly will recall the international tension created by the Cuban missile crisis, when a nuclear war appeared to be a very real threat. The world held its breath as Russia and America confronted one another. For Robert, this confrontation became all he could think about at the time and he was in a highly nervous state. Sleep would not come as he lay awake thinking of the possible consequences of this event. Eventually, he fell into a state of half sleep, but was suddenly awakened and saw to his right a cloud of light forming, growing in intensity. In the midst a figure appeared. A voice in his own mind said, 'Don't worry, the missiles will never be used.' He realised that this was a reference to the missiles dotted around the world and poised so precariously, ready for instant action in the current crisis. On 24 October the five Soviet ships stopped short of the American ships blockading Cuba. Khrushchev backed down and an agreement was forged that he would not erect missiles if the United States would agree not to invade Cuba. The world and Robert breathed easily again.

A second reassuring experience happened to Robert some time later whilst holidaying in Devon, England. One night he was awakened by loud, distant explosions. During the Second World War he had been on the receiving end of a mortar attack, an experience which left him nervous and vulnerable to loud noises. Hearing this explosion he was plunged back into the feelings and the terror that the wartime incident had evoked. Suddenly, the same intense bright light appeared accompanying the figure, and the same voice said, 'Don't worry, there will be no more explosions'.

The next morning Robert discovered that a fire in an arms depot had caused the noise. Once again, he felt flooded with feelings of relief and calm and soon drifted into a deep comfortable sleep.

David's two experiences each feature a voice, one definitely saving his life. The first incident took place when David was 19 years old. Since his late teens he had been interested in church architecture. He loved the varying styles and the stained glass. Hours were spent delving into the nooks and crannies of each new church he visited in Britain and the United States. One day, however, when investigating a deserted building, he found a most interesting spiral staircase. Being intensely curious by nature, he climbed it. It turned steeply for some way, then ended at the top with a locked door. This was too much of an adventure to stop, so David struggled with the lock until he was able to open the door slightly. He gazed on to a flat roof, and immediately thought that this would be in full view of anyone glancing upwards. At this point a voice said firmly, 'If you go out, you will be seen.' He halted, not knowing where the voice in his head had come from, realising also that he should not have opened the door. For fear of discovery, he closed it again and descended the spiral staircase.

He continued his exploration of the church but eventually became curious to see from outside just where the staircase would have led, and where he would be standing if he had gone out. There was no flat roof in evidence anywhere, but in the end he located the door, some 20 feet above the ground in a wall, leading into space. What he had quickly glimpsed and mistaken for a flat roof was the car park below. He would have plunged 20 feet to the ground below, had the voice not warned him. The fear of being seen somewhere he obviously should not have been was the warning to which he had responded.

The second time David heard a warning voice was ten years after the first incident, a very normal type of day containing no apparent danger. He arrived home after a walk, took off his coat, and went into the kitchen to make a snack. A voice came loud and clear: 'If you were a child, you'd be told to wash your hands.' It seemed a simple warning, but David chose to ignore it. After all, he had not been gardening or handling anything dirty, so he went ahead and prepared a sandwich. Only a few hours later, he became violently ill and had good cause to regret that he had ignored the warning – angelic intervention of a most practical kind.

Karen is a very gentle person, with a soft Irish lilt to her voice and a calm, sweet manner. Perhaps that is partly why the same atmosphere comes over in Karen's encounter with angels. She has now received their reassurance many times and it is especially significant that she benefits greatly from the feeling of not being alone. The feeling of protection is powerful for Karen, who needs that reassurance to keep her going through what has been a dreadful time in her life. The first time this help arrived was when she knew it was going to be one of those days. Life had not been easy over the previous 18 months, following on from the day that Karen's husband had stepped into a taxi early one summer morning and headed for the airport on a business trip. It was some hours later that she was told of the fatal motorway accident which deprived her of her beloved Jack and their three children of a very dear father.

Immediately after the accident Karen took the children to her father's home in Belfast, and they tried to pick up the pieces of their formerly happy life. Eventually, back in her own home with the children back at school, life slowly took on a semblance of normality. Twelve months passed and, despite many problems and complications, Karen was coping. At this point, a friend told her about a clairvoyant, a woman who apparently had an amazing gift and insight, and Karen was keen to see her.

The session was astonishing. Facts and details were revealed about her husband that only Karen knew. She was filled with hope in the knowledge that Jack was fine and communicating with her. She felt convinced there was an afterlife and thrilled to hear the clairvoyant say that the message that came from Jack was how proud he was of her to see how well she was coping.

For some time this message provided help and comfort, but inevitably a dark cloud descended. Christmas especially was a struggle, spent once more in her father's home in Belfast. The preparations held little joy for her, and trying to be jolly for the children was quite a strain. It was with some relief that January, school and routine brought back some comfort. With the start of the new year she had become more hopeful, until this particular day. From the moment of waking Karen knew it would be a struggle. Once more her head was filled with the events of the previous eighteen months and all the accompanying stresses and worries.

Struggling with her household chores, she stood in the kitchen feeling despair wash over her, desperate for help. Suddenly she felt a hand on her shoulder and looked around in astonishment. There was no one there and no hand on her shoulder, but the sensation was real enough. Bemused and a little shaken, she made a cup of coffee and sat down to collect her thoughts. She had a feeling of reassurance, that she was not alone and that this hand wanted to say to her, 'Trust'. Some time later she looked through the window and saw a car pull up. From the car appeared the clairvoyant. Karen was once again astonished. There had been no appointment made; the woman did not live in the area and the house was so far off the beaten track that it was most unlikely she was simply passing. Karen opened the door and the clairvoyant said, 'I know you must be surprised to see me, but for some time today I've felt you needed me. You came into my head a little while ago with such clarity I knew I must come.' Karen smiled. At last, it all made sense. She would never in future doubt that there was an angel at her shoulder.

The final experience in this section incorporates almost all the elements of previous encounters we have discussed: rescue, illness, warnings, light, a hand on the shoulder and a crisis. Graham's story would have ended in tragedy were it not for angelic intervention. Graham began diving almost by accident some 15 years ago on holiday in North Wales. On returning home to Cheshire, in the north of England, he made enquiries and found and joined the nearest diving club. Training followed, and eventually Graham was ready for his first dive. This confirmed his belief that he would love the sport and he was hooked. Some time later he met his wife, Sandra, through the club and all their spare time was absorbed with diving. They dreamed of diving in warm waters and sunnier spots on the globe. Hearing of a group of divers planning a trip to Spain, they eagerly joined them and found the sport simply wonderful in the warm conditions.

Several years passed, during which they saved and spent as much time and money as possible travelling to parts of the Mediterranean to dive. One winter's day they saw a travel programme on television about Australia, including a sequence about diving on the Great Barrier Reef. It seemed the ultimate goal for divers and they were determined to reach Australia at all costs. It took a while for plans to formulate and finances to be arranged, but they eventually set out on a three-week holiday to the east coast of Australia. Their wildest dreams were more than fulfilled. Diving off the coast of Australia was an incredible experience, and from day one it became obvious that they would want to stay there. Determined to return, on their arrival home they sold the house and car, and although feeling many pangs at leaving friends and family they never doubted that Australia was to be their new home.

Life was good, until what transpired one Saturday morning in spring, a lovely clear day with the prospect of some diving ahead. They had planned a picnic, but when Graham came into the kitchen to help Sandra prepare breakfast, she complained of feeling a little out of sorts. Graham did feel pangs of disappointment as he was so looking forward to a day outside. Work had prevented them from indulging in their favourite sport for several weeks. Sensing Graham's disappointment, Sandra insisted he went alone, assuring him that she would be fine, having only a headache and wanting to rest. Protesting only slightly, he eventually agreed, saying he would be back in the late afternoon and not be away longer, as they had originally intended.

Taking a packed lunch, Graham went into the garage to load the car with his equipment. The kitchen had a door leading directly into the garage, and he went in and out several times, lifting things he would need into the car. Finally he said goodbye, feeling a little guilty but eager to dive. He stepped into the garage, closing the door behind him. On approaching the car, with his keys ready, he suddenly felt a hand on his shoulder. Turning round, he expected to find Sandra holding some item he'd forgotten, but there was no one there. Standing there for a moment perplexed, he nevertheless ended up deciding that he had imagined the sensation.

Graham went towards the car once more, intending to open the door and drive away, but once again the hand fell on his shoulder. As before he turned around to find nothing, until the darkened garage started to fill with light, so bright and yet so soft that he knew something supernatural was happening. Hurrying through the door back into the house, he called Sandra to tell her what had happened, but there was no response. Dashing into the lounge, he saw her slumped on the floor, her face as white as a sheet. His heart pounding, he felt for a pulse. To his immense relief she was still alive. He quickly called for help and in only minutes, although the wait seemed like hours, they were on the way to hospital.

On arrival, it was discovered that Sandra had suffered a stroke, and Graham was told that the speed at which she had been admitted to hospital had been very much in her favour. Sandra made an excellent recovery. Graham mulls over daily the events of that

Saturday morning, with awe and wonder. He is not, nor ever has been, a religious man, but it had obviously been a case of intervention by an angel, without whose help Sandra would surely have died. Graham says that he wishes he could thank the angel with all his heart, but then, being an angel, he's sure he knows.

FRIENDLY VISITATIONS

We have read accounts of angels appearing in all their splendour, with white wings and light radiating from them. What can we say about angels of normal human appearance? It may in those situations be difficult to say whether it was an angel or not. Swedenborg stressed that the angelic is in all of us. A young girl came to him one day and asked if he would show her an angel. Leading her to his summer house in the garden, he placed her before a closed curtain and said 'Now you shall see an angel.' As he spoke he parted the curtains, so that the young girl saw a reflection of herself in a mirror.

What Leopold experienced also concerns a young girl, whom he met in Sydney, Australia.

'I have felt on a few occasions in my life that angels have been near, but this time I am certain that I actually met one. Most people, myself included, think that angels come in a "mystical" form. They think only of wings, white gowns and bright lights, but my experience tells me otherwise: sometimes they come in the guise of ordinary people. A few years ago I was going through a very difficult patch in my life. I was working very long hours in the Children's Hospital in Sydney, and my mind was constantly in a turmoil.

'This incident happened on a Sunday afternoon, while I was involved in a piece of work at the Hospital's Outpatients Centre, in a corridor which led off the main reception area, where a handful of people were waiting to see a doctor. I was attending to my work, when out of nowhere there appeared, about ten metres away, a tall, handsome man with a little girl, walking slowly up the corridor towards me. Initially I didn't take much notice, but when they were about three metres away I stopped working and looked up, straight into the face of the little girl. She smiled at me, but although I would normally talk easily to people and children, I found that I could not say anything. I smiled back, however, and more to myself than to her I mumbled, "You are so beautiful, you are an angel." There really was something angelic about her.

'I returned to my work, but still felt strange, repeating to myself, "You are an angel". I had to kneel down at this point to carry on with my work, and I smiled at the child. The next thing I knew, the little girl came to me, stretched out her hand, and gave me a kiss on my cheek. I was mesmerised. Children don't normally do things like this to strangers; all I could say was "Thank you" and again, "You are an angel." She was so sweet.

'I turned back to my work and did not carry on watching, assuming that she would go back to her father and that they would be walking back the way they came. I was stunned, unable to understand why I was so affected emotionally. I looked up again as they walked through the doorway into the reception area. This had all taken less than a minute. I now started to realise that I wanted to talk to them, to tell the father how sweet she was and maybe give her a hug as a thank you. I followed them into reception; still no more than a minute or two had elapsed since they had left me. They were nowhere to be seen. I went outside, but still there was no sign of them. In fact, there were no other people around, everywhere was quiet. I went back inside and asked the receptionist if she had seen them or if they had gone to see a doctor, but she said no. A nurse then appeared and I asked her too if she had seen the man with the little girl, but she replied, "No". I checked everywhere I could again, but there was no sign of them.

'I am still puzzled about this incident, being a practical, logical person, and it is a mystery to me how they could have disappeared so quickly. It must have been an angel, maybe bringing the message that with love we can survive.'

Like Claire, many of us first heard of angels in Sunday School when very young. The teacher told the class that everyone had a guardian angel given to them at birth, who would be with them and look after them until the day they died. They were told that if they were good children their angel was happy, but if they were naughty, their angel would put its head in its hands and cry. This had made a big impression on Claire at the time, and for a short while she was very conscious of having a special 'friend'. Unfortunately, as is the way with children, this was a nine-day wonder, and her mind was soon filled with other things.

Many years passed, until in 1984 Claire had an encounter with an angel.

'I was working as a companion to an old lady of 90 in a residential home for the elderly. Polly was a lovely lady and, most of the time, very easy to look after. However, at certain times she was very difficult to control. On this particular morning, I was having great difficulty getting her out of bed, washed and dressed. I could see her spiralling completely out of control, and I was at the end of my tether. I was standing in front of her, as she sat on the side of the bed and I said, in a very exasperated voice, "Oh, Polly, for goodness' sake!" That was as far as I got, because I suddenly saw behind her a blue-white light that, as I looked, seemed to be in the shape of wings folded around her. Then a voice, full of compassion, said, "Oh, soul, soul, this isn't really me. I'm not like this."

'It's difficult to describe the feeling. It seemed such a natural thing. I accepted it quietly, and suddenly everything seemed at peace. The light disappeared, Polly was very calm and I was very quiet. I didn't rush out and tell anyone about my experience. I wanted to keep it to myself, a private happening. It was only when I went home that I told my husband Robin what had happened. I remember he smiled. We didn't make a big thing about it; we just accepted and believed. In the last two years, angels seem to have been making their presence felt, as though nudging my elbow to let me know they were there.'

ANGELS OF LIGHT

Light features strongly in many reports of angels. It is also a key aspect of the near-death experience and many books on this subject emphasise this by having the word 'light' in their titles. For example, Dr Cherie Sutherland, an Australian researcher, called her book *Within the Light*. She reports many encounters, including the experience of someone who felt the light surround her and was aware of a circle of hands reaching out to her through the light. Although John did not have an NDE, he was certainly at a point of crisis, and he was powerfully affected by the light.

For most of John's adult life he has had a profound

feeling of spirituality, without being religious. A few years ago, after a heart-breaking end to his marriage, he began a slide into a deep depression and physical decline, until he was eventually taken into hospital. Feelings of panic swept over him but although medical staff tried to help, nothing seemed to work. John felt their efforts were unwelcome, and he wished mainly to be left alone.

One day he woke in what he describes as a state of darkness. He felt great fear, and the sensation of being on the edge of a precipice. He stood by his hospital bed, quite unable to move. The blackness of his spirit was matched by a physical blackness, for in his panic he found that he could not see. This was the most frightening episode in John's entire life. Totally at a loss as to what was happening, scared of stepping forward because of the terrifying blackness, he nevertheless fought against his panic. Suddenly, an inner voice told him to turn around, to circle away mentally and physically from the dark abyss he feared. The voice intensified. Gathering all the courage he could find within, John forced himself to turn around. He was at once engulfed in the brightest light he had ever seen or could possibly imagine, but not hurting the eyes at all. The feelings accompanying this light were hard to articulate, but love was predominant. The darkness was gone and John could start on the road to a complete recovery.

A bubble of light is yet another image people use to try and explain the feeling of being completely surrounded, externally and internally, by this angelic light. Richard tells of being engulfed within the light, and is able to ask questions, and receive answers from 'beings of light'. This story begins in south-east London, in a university hall of residence in October 1991. Richard was away from home for the first time, enjoying the freedom. As with all students, the problems of spinning out his grant and worrying about girlfriends were uppermost in his mind, and Richard began to struggle to cope with his studies. However, after a while he made two special friends in Victoria and Sarah. The friendship with Sarah was to prove particularly significant in the following events. She appeared to have not only a life mapped out, and motivation, but also inner peace. She seemed to have a direct channel to something higher.

One evening, deep in discussion, Sarah said that she could feel something taking place. Richard felt a tremendous surge of energy and elation, surrounded by and absorbed in a feeling of pure love. A huge bubble of intense white light surrounded him, and he became aware of a voice within the light. He was able to ask questions and receive answers, and he was aware that he was communicating with beings of a higher consciousness. The experience was so intense that it was three or four months before he felt he was wholly back in reality. His life has completely changed, and he now has the direction and peace of mind he so urgently sought.

ANGELS IN DREAMS

For thousands of years people have believed their dreams to be significant. Dream interpretation was prominent in ancient Egypt, where you could go to a library and look up an interpretation of your dream. The Bible contains many examples of dreams featuring angels. In Genesis, for instance, there is a striking story of Jacob as a young man having a dream in which he saw a staircase joining heaven to earth. Angels were ascending and descending upon it. This could be interpreted today as levels of consciousness leading us to God. It is powerful symbolism and relevant for us here and now. We, like the angels in the dream, have to aspire to higher levels.

I have included the following account not just because angels appear in it, but because dreams, like angels, can convey messages to us from higher realms. The dream Carole relates had a clarity that remains with her still.

'Several years ago I was working in a large insurance office in the centre of Manchester. The work could be rather routine, but I was fortunate enough to work with a group of extremely nice people. The eldest group member, Leslie, was perhaps the most likeable character of them all. Quietly spoken, yet a cheery character, he also had an amusing dry sense of humour. The two great passions in his life were his family and an old dog called Fudge. It was a sad day when Leslie retired, and we all missed him a great deal.

'Not long after Leslie's retirement, my husband was transferred to another part of the country and I left the office. Feeling lost at first, I soon became involved with a new community. When my son was born, I began to meet other new mothers and various groups, busy with a new life. I kept in touch with Leslie, but inevitably contact dwindled to a Christmas card containing a hurried note. Several years passed, and it was only when my Christmas card list emerged that I would think about Leslie. However, one hot July night I had a powerfully vivid dream about Leslie.

'The dream portrayed him in heaven, with an angel on either side of him, beaming and shining with light, with almost iridescent robes. Leslie was also dressed in white, smiling and looking extremely happy. He raised his arm and waved to me. Gradually all three figures faded, replaced by a beautiful landscape. I woke to find it morning. Amazed and confused by the vividness of the dream, I did in fact wonder if I hadn't been dreaming at all and had really seen the figures. Sliding out of bed, I pulled on my dressing gown and pottered downstairs to make a cup of tea, still wondering why Leslie should feature so prominently in a dream in the middle of summer. I reached the bottom stair and saw a letter lying on the doormat. It was addressed to me in an unfamiliar handwriting, and bore a Manchester post-mark. Intrigued, I opened it quickly and gasped, for it was a letter from Leslie's wife, telling me he had died two days previously.'

ANGELS IN ART AND POPULAR CULTURE

It seems that angels pervade every aspect of life, and always have done. If we look at art forms, both ancient and modern, we see a great angelic influ-ence. Many cultures and religions refer to angels, and the images evolve over the years. Painting features sig-nificantly in the following story.

Jean was literally touched by an angel, a profound and unexpected encounter. She was 22 at the time, and she begins her story by setting the scene.
'I was living on a narrowboat moored in the side-stream off the River Thames in Oxford, England. One summer's morning I woke as usual and lay for a while, enjoying the gentle rocking of my oversized cradle. I was in the middle of planning my day when I suddenly became aware of the presence of someone inside the boat. I told myself that it couldn't be so, because the motion of the boat had not changed and there had been no lurch as there would have to be if someone stepped on board. However, I had the feeling we have when we

sense someone behind us and turn around to find that they are watching us – only many times more power-ful. Still not fully accepting this presence, I felt it move towards me, floating in the air. Then it was above me, and the atmosphere seemed to press down on me very slightly, as if something was taking up the space. All at once I saw clearly within my inner vision a woman with long flowing hair and a very wise, kindly feel about her. The next moment, she reached down and covered my hand with hers. Her hand was solid, slightly cooler than mine, firm, yet gentle. I was paralysed with primi-tive fear. Two long seconds – and then her hand was gone, and with it went her presence and my fear. In its place I experienced a great sense of reassurance, know-ing that someone was there for me. I did not share this experience with anyone for ten years, for fear of being ridiculed. I just quietly knew I had my "guardian angel", as I called her.

'Ten years later, I came across someone I could tell, and I made my first painting of her. This was subse-quently stolen by someone whose need for the paint-ing must have been greater than mine, and I was eventually able to let it go mentally, and paint a new version – which I much preferred. This one has now gone to someone else too, bought by a friend. Also, after many years of fondly remembering my experi-ence, I began to realise I could call my guardian angel and she would come. The first time this happened, I found myself unexpectedly walking home alone in the dark. Faced with the prospect of a pathway that led up and away from the road and under shadowy trees, I felt more than slightly frightened. I stood still and remembered my guardian angel, wishing she was there. As I wished, I felt a most wonderful, relaxing, gentle glow at my back – and knew that she was there. I walked up that hill with the greatest ease, without a single fearful thought in my mind, singing all the way!

'Now she is with me whenever I call her. And interestingly, letters I have since received regarding reproductions of my "Guardian Angel" painting always describe how this picture has brought great comfort, especially to those in particular need of help and healing. I am sure each one of us has our own guardian angel.'

Much poetry has been inspired by angels. Sylvia did not write a poem, but her cloud (described below) has a creative, almost poetic quality. Here is a short story, set in spring, the description of a day full of new beginnings.

'It was one of those perfect spring days. The sky was a deep blue and the blossom was floating on the trees. I was standing in my bedroom gazing through the window, enjoying the beautiful view. I was truly counting my blessings and there seemed to be more than ever that wonderful morning. I started to think about a programme I had seen on television about personal experiences with angels on which several people had related fascinating experiences. Looking through the window, I noticed one huge cumulus cloud in the middle of the sky, surrounded by deep blue. There was not a breath of wind and it hung there motionless.

'At this point I closed my eyes and started to pray, not as one frequently does, asking for help or out of stress, but a prayer of gratitude for all the beauty and my happiness. It was a prayer so intense I felt directly connected and at peace. Opening my eyes I gasped in astonishment, for the huge cloud had formed itself into the shape of an angel. Two enormous wings fanned out and reached above a perfectly formed head. There were even breaks in the cloud to produce two blue eyes. The body flowed down and tapered away. I stood mesmerised by this fabulous formation. There was still not the slightest breeze and no indication of movement whatsoever. Frequently I close my eyes and see again my cloud angel. It was a truly awesome experience.'

When we consider the history of painting in Western Europe, we see various styles in the depiction of angelic beings. In medieval times, the splendour of multicoloured and many-layered wings is remarkable. Later comes Baroque richness, with cherubs a-plenty. Blake's angels were powerfully portrayed, while the Pre-Raphaelite angels were different again but still of great beauty.

Nowadays, angels appear in painting, film, sculpture, music and literature. The influence is strong in pop music. The Eurythmics sang about 'an angel playing with my heart'. Kate Bush has two such tracks on her album *The Red Shoes*, and the Abba hit *I Have a Dream* is remembered by most people mainly for the chorus: 'I believe in angels, something good in everything I see'. Paul McCartney has said that the music for one of his most famous songs *Yesterday* was planted in his mind one night, and he woke up the next morning still remembering it. I wonder if this was a gift from the angels. It seems significant that he later called his band Wings.

Cinema and television, barometers of popular culture, show signs that the modern world has not discarded angels. *Ghost* was a big hit, where the main character becomes a guardian angel for his wife after he dies. Audrey Hepburn in *Always* contrasts with Paul Hogan in an Australian angel role in *Almost an Angel*. The German director Wim Wenders made the thought-provoking *Wings of Desire* and its sequel *Far Away So Close*. Television has many examples, but a prominent one is *Quantum Leap*, in which miraculous powers and angelic functions are given to a human being through time travel.

The Victorians loved angels, who were especially popular at the turn of the century. (Is it a coincidence that interest is growing as we approach the millennium?) Angel monuments to their loved ones were erected in graveyards and became an art form in themselves.

Large numbers of people may soon be influenced by the work of the sculptor Antony Gormley, in Gateshead in the north-east of England. Even in its early stages, this project has provoked strong reactions. Mike White, Arts Officer for Gateshead Council, tells us more of this attempt to create an angel which is not 'conventional' or 'fluffy', as he puts it (and his views expressed below are not necessarily those of the Council).

'We are not talking here so much about seeing an angel, as about producing one. In Gateshead we are making a colossal steel angel. Towering above the A1 motorway on the ridge of the Tyne valley, 20 metres tall with a wingspan of 52 metres, the Angel of the North, by internationally renowned sculptor Antony Gormley, will be built in 1996 as the culmination of the UK Visual Arts Year. Constructed from a weathering steel, it will be a welcoming landmark for 150 years and the single largest piece of public art in Britain – if in the next few months we can achieve the massive funding package required for its production.* I have been working on this project for two years already, and have learned the virtue of optimism when it comes to building an angel.

*As this book went to press, The Angel of the North received the full funding package sought from the National Lottery and the European Regional Development Fund. Fabrication of the Angel is expected to commence in a north-east shipyard in the autumn and the sculpture will be erected on site in the spring of 1997.

'Part of my need to remain optimistic has come from the amount of opposition to this project. As a local government arts officer, I am well used to the controversy that can descend on contemporary works of public art. But I was surprised by the furore that emerged in the crucial stage of obtaining planning permission for this sculpture, despite the proven success in Gateshead of a ten-year public art programme with community involvement. An angel, it seems, is the most provocative of images. As the poet Rilke recognised, angels can inspire terror or euphoria. In the course of attempting to achieve the Council's ambitious wishes to realise this sculpture at no direct cost to local people, there have been some dark hours personally. Yet through it I have made valuable new friends with whom I communicate via angels, pictorially and in spirit. I have yet to have a paranormal encounter but the Angel of the North is certainly a paranormal project in public art terms!

'This is not a conventional fluffy angel but an industrial one, with its cased metal wings outstretched from an "Everyman" figure in a gesture of embrace and vulnerability that belies the sculpture's strength. Critics, loosely grouped through the activities of the local press into an "anti-statue coalition", have variously decried Gormley's Angel as a waste of money, a hazard to traffic, an unbuildable structure, a fascist monument, a disruptor of TV signals and aircraft navigation systems, and even as a blasphemy. Urban myths abound. The

Angel's supporters, a growing but quieter con-
stituency of interests, are more concerned with its
down-to-earth but multi-layered symbolism, seeing it
as a heritage-free emblem of Tyneside's proud engineering past and a portent of the enduring value of
human labour among a highly skilled industrial community with a passion for celebration.

'Ove Arup and Partners, arguably the best struc-
tural engineers in the world, have concluded that the
Angel can be built, and much of the symbolism of the
emblem comes out in the physical structure. Eighty
tons of steel wings hovering above a gale-swept ridge
top will bear down on the Angel's ankles, rooted into a
mound and foundations where a colliery bath house
once stood. It will stand at the end of a field where the
Great Strike miners' meetings took place in Victorian
times and in the 1920s. The Angel's architectural
strength comes from the use of an external rib structure which passes on the strain on the figure from the
wind into the ground through a series of interlocking
plates. The Angel is thus an anchorage, but with the
imminent and ever-present suggestion of flight, sym-
bolising the transcendent anchored into the earthly
and everyday. Similarly, in the rib structure – a kind of
inverted ship's hull – the engineering and aesthetic
solutions fuse together.'

Some of sculptor Antony Gormley's thoughts on the
structure and its site are included below. His design
was selected by Gateshead Council from an interna-

tional shortlist of artists' proposals. The location and context for the Angel have drawn on Gormley's fascination for the human form writ large in monumental but non-heroic sculpture. Its form comes out of the featureless bodycast techniques and contemplative casings (in which he often takes mouldings of his own body) which have become Gormley's trademarks.

'The hilltop site is important and has the feeling of being a megalithic mound. When you think of the mining that was done underneath the site there is a poetic resonance. Men worked beneath the surface in the dark. Now, in the light, there is a celebration and visibility of this industry. The Angel spans two realms – heavenly and earthly – and is an expression of the continuity of life. The steel will be a rust-red, rich brown colour, the colour of earth and blood. The face will not have individual features. The effect of the piece is in the alertness, the awareness of space, and the gesture of the wings. It will be one of the largest single-object pieces built in the last 20 years. Don't you think people are going to talk about it and want to see it?'

Mike White continues:

'An education programme to accompany the sculpture commission is already underway in local schools, covering the symbolism of angels, the engineering of art, bodycasting, and a collaborative artwork made by Gormley with a cross-section of Gateshead's population. The artist is also taking part in a series of debates with theologians at Durham Cathedral.

'A sub-culture is also emerging around the sculpture. The Sunday football team which plays by the site has renamed itself 'the Angels'. Poems and jokes about angels abound in local newspaper columns. Even the bitterest critics (often motivated by local politics) have found some creative strand to their outrage. It has become a huge conversation piece – even before it is built.

'The Angel will be fabricated in the north-east with most of the money going to support local heavy industry. The longer term benefits will come through tourism and an angelic image to promote our region through the next millennium. The sculpture will be encountered daily by 90,000 passing vehicles and by passengers on the London to Edinburgh east-coast rail line. Sited in a panoramic landscape characterised by rapid motion and natural stillness, the Angel of the North will celebrate the abundance of creative energy and industrial material which goes beyond mere function. Like a true spiritual being it exists both within and beyond the confining spirit of our time. This seems to be a good time to be making an angel. So, fingers crossed – "Hallelujah", "Hosanna" and other lucky words from the great lexicon of angels.'

Through the Eyes of a Child

Thou, suspending thy flight,
mayst see another child for tending

ROBERT BROWNING

One of the joys in writing this book has been the privilege of talking to children. They talk about angels and their experiences in a very matter-of-fact way, with an air of surprise that they even have to spell out the details. They are so open and willing to encounter angels and receive their help. Adults, reliving childhood encounters with angels, also tell of how easily they accepted these events.

The V.E. Day 50th anniversary celebrations brought back early memories for Elsie. Even though she was a child at the time, certain events made an indelible impression on her mind. She lived on the outskirts of Manchester in a pleasant suburban area, with pretty gardens and neat, semi-detached houses. However, not too far away was a large industrial estate containing factories vital for the war effort and, as such, a prime target for bombers from Germany. She was a nervous child and not happy in the dark, so the war years were a trial for her, with the noise and the blackout.

Elsie was about six or seven one stiflingly hot summer. She would dread bedtimes, when she had to lie in a hot, stuffy room, with the blackout curtains pulled down tightly. She did, however, enjoy waking, pulling up those dreaded blinds and seeing the silvery-grey barrage balloons floating above the park. Her child's perception was that they were there to cheer her up during such scary times.

Elsie's parents tried hard to make life as normal as possible, but, inevitably, the sirens would wail and they would be bustled out of the house to an air-raid shelter. Despite her parents' efforts to make light of it all for her benefit, Elsie became increasingly fearful, especially of bed-time. This is what happened one particular night, as summer became especially hot and bed-time more and more of an ordeal.

'That evening I was in floods of tears. I begged my mother not to pull down the awful black blind and to leave the window slightly open. She relented and said that just for once I could look through the window but I had to promise not to switch on the light. I agreed happily, but sleep refused to come and I climbed out of bed still shaking from the sobs and fright. Suddenly there was the most beautiful sight I have ever seen, a figure of light floating outside the window, two huge white wings and such a lovely face smiling at me, shining from head to toe. All my fear vanished as I stood gazing at the being of light. In a moment she was gone, but I was left with a sense of security and a feeling that all would be well.

'At breakfast I told my parents who murmured something about a lovely dream, but I knew only too well that I had been awake. Years later I saw a book with illustrations of angels, and I realised my beautiful experience had brought me face to face with an angel. I had never seen or heard of angels until then and it was a great surprise to see that the drawing in the book exactly matched what I had seen that night. From that night on I was no longer afraid, going to bed and sleeping with ease. To this day I have a feeling of being watched over and cared for by my guardian angel.'

Feelings of love and safety shine through the next account. We are reminded that all of us, and children especially, matter a great deal to the angels. They act *in loco parentis* on occasions, it seems, and the protection they offer is evidence that we all have a guardian angel.

One night stands out vividly in Susan's childhood memories. She was four years old, and had been settled in bed by her baby-sitter. Her parents led fairly busy lives. Her father, a railway worker, frequently worked at night, and on this particular night her mother was also away from home attending a ladies' meeting in the church hall. For some time Susan had been troubled with nightmares and disturbed sleep-patterns. On this occasion, this obviously led to sleep-walking, which, in turn, led to this angelic encounter.

'I vividly recall waking in my parents' room, curled up before an open fire. I was lying on the floor at the end of my parents' bed, dangerously close to the burning coals. It's difficult to describe the sequence of events that followed. I was clearly in that limbo between sleep and reality, but I distinctly felt the sensation of being lifted by gentle hands. I recall retaining the same crouched, curled position and feeling slightly frightened as I literally floated back to my own bed. Gently, I was placed into the bed. My eyes were tightly shut but I could feel the covers being pulled over me. There was no one in the room, no voice, but such a tremendous feeling of safety, peace and love surrounding me. The hands that lifted me were not human hands. The floating, the intense feelings of peace and love to me indicate only one explanation – I had been visited by an angel.'

What follows is an account of two sisters and their connection with angels. There are two stories about this family, but the second appears later in the book. The first story is about a little girl, and I always think of this event as the flight of angels. Many years ago, when I lived in Los Angeles, in one inner-city area there was a very steep hill connecting two streets, one at the top and the other at the bottom. The incline was so sharp that between the two a funicular had been built. Rising from one level to the other was great fun. It provided a wonderful view and was very easy on the legs. The project was called 'Flight of Angels'. Sadly, it was dismantled when a new building scheme engulfed it. The funicular was put into storage with a promise of restoration one day. Years later it still waits to be released from the ever-increasing rust.

Let us return to the two sisters and their story. As children, Paniyota and her sister, Vaghoulla, lived on the beautiful island of Cyprus in a small village called Galata, with their close-knit family of three sisters and two brothers. Each evening the three sisters would eat their supper and then go up the stairs to bed together. Vaghoulla, the youngest sister, would climb ahead, skipping and always waving into the darkness. One night Paniyota asked, 'What are you waving at?' and Vaghoulla replied, 'The lovely angels of course.' She then saw her sisters' astonished faces and realised for the first time that they could not see them. To their amazement Vaghoulla said that every night as she climbed the stairs three pretty cherubs were waiting and flew up alongside her, smiling and waving. She would wave back, feeling happy and safe, and assuming her sisters saw them also. The sad part of this story is that from the night the sisters learned of the cherubs' presence they never appeared to Vaghoulla again.

Anyone who remembers beach holidays as a child will identify with this story and the agony of having to go home and leave the beach, no matter how tired the sun, sea and fresh air had made you. The idea of bed was abhorrent. Even though Janet lived just above the beach, the family home being on the Gower Peninsula in south-west Wales, these feelings were just as strong in her.

'One beautiful warm evening, after a day on the beach, dinner and a long chat with family, especially Grandma, who was staying for a few weeks, I went to bed very happy, but as far from sleep as any child could possibly be. The sky was still light and I could not bring myself to climb into the bed. I sat looking through the window down to the sea. The window was open and the smell of seaweed wafted through on the breeze. Although I knew it was forbidden, I decided to go out and sneak down to the beach for one last look at the shells. I had been told not to wander alone after dinner and certainly not to venture down to the sea without adults. Slipping out of the back door in sandals and pyjamas, I felt as if I were heading for a great adventure. Excited and fearful, knowing that what I was doing was disobedient, I slowly crept to the path. It was as if I was compelled to go on. It came as rather a surprise on reaching the bottom of the path to find the beach submerged. It had not occurred to me that the tide would be in. Totally unaware of the time passing, I did not know how long I had been away from the house and day-dreaming by the sea, but the sun had almost set and the sky was on the point of darkening.

'I seemed to be aware almost at once that I must hurry back or I should find myself alone in the dark. This thought frightened me so much that I jumped up and immediately lost my footing, my sandal slipping on the wet step. In an instant I was in the sea. Fortunately it was not deep at this point and I had my feet on the lower submerged steps, but I was soaking wet and shivering as I hauled myself out. Even though the day had been hot, the sea was still cold and the air now chilly and I was very frightened and very wet. I had to negotiate the steep path in the half-light and tears came flooding down my face in despair. My right sandal was missing and my pyjamas were wet through, making the ascent of the beach path very difficult. Slipping in panic, I lay sobbing on the ground, appalled at my own stupidity.

'Suddenly, I felt a wonderful warmth and a glowing light all around me. It was as if a spotlight was shining on me from above. Looking up, I saw a beautiful lady shining with light, with bright hair and a long white dress. She gave me a loving, encouraging smile and I got to my feet, only to find myself at the *very top* of the path. In my confusion I wondered if my bright lady had carried me up the path, but could not recall any sensation of being lifted or movement of any kind. I could see my house, lights shining on to the lawn, and a feeling of security enveloped me. No word was spoken, but the beautiful lady raised her hand and faded away. If I had not been dripping wet, I might have thought I'd imagined or dreamed the whole episode.

'Quickly I ran home, bursting through the back door to find an astonished mother and grandmother sitting at the kitchen table. They had been unaware that I had even left the house, and I know for sure that the roasting I then received was not imagined! After they had calmed down and I had had a hot drink, I told the whole story. It often seems like yesterday, so clear is it in my mind, but it was in fact some 20 years ago when I was six or seven years old. I have often thought about the incident, and the only conclusion I can draw is that the lady was my guardian angel. Thank goodness, I haven't needed her again like that since that night, but I feel quite strongly that she is never far away.'

This next story might never have come to light, had Jonathan's mother not asked the routine question, 'What did you see?' on his return from a school trip. As mentioned earlier, children are very matter-of-fact regarding the supernatural and take it in their stride. Jonathan was no exception, and his common-sense telling of the events of that day is typical of children's attitudes.

Jonathan was one of three children in a loving family. The home he shared with his sisters and parents was spacious and comfortable. He enjoyed school and had many friends. In short, life was sunny. One day his world was turned upside down, when he lost his much loved father. Many questions followed, some very difficult for his grieving mother to answer, but he carried on bravely attending school, though often saying how much he wished he could see his father one more time.

Some weeks after the funeral the school was preparing to close for the long summer break. Jonathan was to go to Ireland to stay with his aunt, along with his mother and sisters. Staying with his aunt had always been great fun. She had lots of space and green fields full of animals, which he loved to help look after. Before this, however, there would be the end-of-term trip, and it was decided that, although he was feeling apprehensive about it, Jonathan should go with his schoolfriends. The school had decided to visit a theme park, and on a hot July day they set out in coaches to spend the day at Gulliver's World.

The day was a great success, and Jonathan arrived home tired but full of the day's events. When his mother asked, 'What did you see?' he answered, 'I saw my Daddy.' His mother, trying to sound calm, asked, 'Where did you see him?' He told her that in a darkened passage in one of the park's attractions his Daddy had appeared, dressed in blue. 'Did he say anything to you?' his mother asked. 'No,' he replied. 'He just smiled, came to me and put his arms around me. I could see him, Mummy, but I couldn't feel him.'

This is the first example we have seen of a relative who has died appearing to someone. There will be more examples of this towards the end of the book, which perhaps bring out more strongly the angelic dimension to this type of experience. In Jonathan's case he does not talk about an angel but the fact that he could see but not feel his father suggests otherwise. The way his father hugs him also suggests something of the desire to give comfort which we associate with angels. At the same time, we are also reminded of Swedenborg's assertion that the angels close to us are people like us who have passed on to another life.

Children experiencing the presence of angels describe bright lights, shining eyes, and the colour of their gowns. Adults describe feelings of love and peace in addition, but although children may experience these also, they find them difficult to articulate.

Jean's account differs from others' in that she felt great fear, and indeed fear has been the abiding memory of that night. This has been unusual in my research, for in other instances, even if fear has been felt initially, more comforting feelings have then developed.

The story related by Jean happened when she was a six-year-old child living in Oxford, England. Next door to Jean lived a little girl of the same age called Amy, and they became firm friends. Constantly visiting the house next-door and even occasionally staying overnight, Jean was happy with her new friend.

One night, while sleeping in Amy's house, she woke suddenly in the early hours to find an angel sitting on her bed. The figure was in profile, and bathed in a whitish-grey light, sitting perfectly still like a marble statue. Jean was very frightened, but reasoned that she might be dreaming. So she shut her eyes tightly, and hoped that on opening them the angel would be gone. However, this was not the case, for when she did open her eyes the angel was still there, motionless as before. Jean was terrified and this time yelled out as loudly as she could for Amy's mother. By the time Amy's mother had woken up and arrived in Jean's room, the figure had faded away. She comforted her and told Jean it was just a dream. Jean, however, is convinced to this day that it was not, so real and vivid is the memory even now, not to mention the fear she experienced.

Angels can be described by children as lovely ladies or people they have known who have died, as glowing with light or even statue-like figures who impart fear, as we have just seen. Kate's angel left her puzzled. There doesn't seem to be any obvious reason for her to have witnessed this angel. Kate was not in need of rescue or distressed in any way – quite the contrary. She was enjoying a morning walk with her grandmother. Kate is now in her early twenties, and still sees no obvious explanation for this episode.

The following event took place when Kate was

eleven years old. It happened in a beautiful part of the British Isles, Falmouth in the county of Cornwall. One morning, Kate and her grandmother were walking into Falmouth. As they drew level with a local church, Kate peeped over the wall into the church grounds. There, to her astonishment, she saw a tall, brightly glowing figure, with the appearance of being lit from within. A halo of fair hair surrounded his head and deep blue eyes stared from a long, pale face. A full, pale-blue gown flowed down to and covered his feet. He seemed to be floating about a foot above the ground. Kate stared in disbelief at this figure appearing before her in broad daylight. Seconds later the figure started to disappear, but it seemed a much longer time than that to Kate. She ran to her grandmother, who was walking only slightly ahead of her, anxious to draw her attention to the figure, but by the time her grandmother turned around it had faded completely. Kate can think of no apparent reason for this event, and has not seen an angel since, but the memory is vivid and clear to this day.

Swedenborg believed that angels are not in a statically perfect state. Although they are highly developed spiritually compared to us, they continue to evolve on a spiritual level. He believed firmly that they are people who have gone before us as trailblazers and who have a great openness to God, which they want to share with us. Another way of seeing them is as our older brothers and sisters. This seems particularly relevant in our next account, in which Jonathan is comforted by a 'big brother angel'. Jonathan was keen to stress, as he talked to me about this happening, that the memory was vivid and fresh in his mind, totally unlike any dreams from childhood, which have faded with the years.

'I was 11 years old and beside myself with excitement at the prospect of a holiday under canvas. It was to be my first holiday without my family; twenty boys and four teachers from my school were to spend a week walking, climbing, canoeing and, weather permitting, swimming in the Lake District. As the Easter holidays approached, my excitement grew to fever pitch and I checked over and over again the things I needed to take. At last the day dawned and we set off in a small coach, waving to our rather apprehensive looking parents. As it turned out, my parents had a reason to be worried!

'The holiday was all I'd hoped for; living in a tent was glorious and so was the weather. The first Saturday arrived and a camp fire was planned, with sausages and lots of singing. I was feeling rather tired at this point, but having spent most nights giggling instead of sleeping, this was only to be expected. To my surprise, when supper arrived I was not at all hungry, in fact I was feeling pretty unwell. As the evening wore on, a pain developed in my stomach and grew increasingly intense. Eventually a teacher became concerned and as

I then became violently sick, it was decided to take me to the nearest hospital. It was unclear exactly how long this took, but it must have been something of a nightmare, driving along twisting roads with the pain becoming worse all the time. The events which followed are somewhat hazy, but it was decided on arrival at hospital that my appendix was the problem. It would have to be removed at once and there were severe complications.

'On waking in a hospital bed, I felt desperately ill, sensing even at that age, with no knowledge of what was happening to me, that there was a strong possibility that I might die. I thought of my parents and wondered if they were on their way, reflecting on how worried they must be feeling. From then on I must have drifted in and out of consciousness, because I remember coming to on several occasions to find a nurse making a check on how I was.

'At one point I opened my eyes and saw a young boy sitting on my bed. He was at the side of the bed, quite close to me, with fair hair and very blue eyes, and he seemed to glow. I couldn't imagine where he'd come from, but I noticed the whole room growing brighter. It all felt very unreal. I remember so very clearly asking him, "Am I going to die?" and he answered, "No, you mustn't worry, everything will be alright." To my amazement, he then literally faded away, the bright light dimmed, and the room returned to its previous low level of lighting. What had changed, however, was that I felt comforted.

'Some time later I woke to find my parents by my bedside, and I realised it was daylight. I was feeling stronger and happy to see those well loved faces. Much later, I told my mother of the little boy and she suggested I might have been dreaming, but I doubt a dream would have made such a lasting impression. It all happened some 15 years ago, but is as clear in my mind now as the night when these events took place. The feelings of comfort and security are with me still.'

Often when people experience something in their lives they find difficult to explain, perhaps especially when it happens in childhood, it is only with hindsight that they believe these events to be angelic intervention.

Throughout Stephanie's life an unseen hand or hands have helped her in moments of danger, stress and confusion. It had not occurred to her that angels would intervene without the sight of beautiful wings and long, white gowns. A hand on her shoulder did not equate with her idea of angelic presence. Only later in life, when she had been helped many times, did she feel that this was indeed her guardian angel. The first of these occasions, she now feels, was when she was six years old, during a family holiday in Blackpool in the north of England.

'We arrived at our hotel and, to my delight, we

were directly opposite the beach. The next day surpassed all my expectations, blue sky and warm sun with a glittering sea. The donkeys seemed to be nodding in my direction, and having to sit down and eat breakfast was torture. At last, we were ready to go. Clutching my sparkling new bucket and spade, I raced down the hotel steps. Behind me, my mother was carrying my baby brother, while behind them my father was carrying all the bags and other bits and pieces. With sheer exuberance I rushed headlong towards the promenade. Heavy trams were clattering up and down, besides the usual seaside traffic, but all I could see was the sand, as I rushed towards the edge of the pavement.

'As I was about to leap into the road, directly in the path of an oncoming tram, I felt a restraining hand on my shoulder. I almost fell with the force of being pulled backwards. Turning, I expected to see my father with a very angry face, but there was no one behind me. My parents were frozen to the spot in horror, still on the hotel steps, and the nearest pedestrian was yards away. I was puzzled and received a severe ticking off, but I couldn't imagine what had happened to me. Eventually, the incident faded from my mind.

'A few years later, when I was just coming up to 11 years old, I moved house and started at a new school. This was a frightening experience and not made any happier by the fact that the children at my new school were rather hostile. Several girls in particular started to bully me. The bullying fell short of actual physical violence, but they made my life miserable, and I felt that violence was bubbling under the surface. I said nothing to anybody, and hoped they would soon grow bored with taunting a new girl.

'Leaving school each day, I had to walk down a rather narrow, dingy street to reach the busy main road and catch the bus home. The days were growing shorter and it was quite dark when I left school. One afternoon I had stayed at school a little later to enrol for a gym club, hoping I might make friends with other girls holding a similar interest. As I left, I noticed that the street was almost deserted. Turning left as usual to walk down the narrow street, I felt a hand on my shoulder. I span round of course, but there was nobody there. Perplexed, but strangely feeling no fear, I set off once more, but again the hand on my shoulder pulled me back. Not understanding what this meant I nevertheless felt it was a warning, and I quickly walked in the opposite direction. I had absolutely no idea where I was going, nor how I should get back to the main road and the bus home. Suddenly, a car pulled up and the horn sounded. I realised that it was our next-door neighbour. She laughed, opening the passenger door and said, "Jump in, Stephanie, you're going in the wrong direction." With great relief, I climbed in and we drove past the school and down the little narrow street. As we did so, however, I saw, hiding in the dark doorway, my tormentors. Their faces on recognising me were filled with disbelief. They had obviously been waiting for me, and who knows what they had in mind?

'I told my mother and my new neighbour about this on arriving home, and to my joy she said she passed the school around that time daily and would be happy to bring me home. Strangely enough, however, I was never troubled by those girls again.

'My adult life has produced at least three incidents where the hand on my shoulder was a saving action. None of these, however, were situations of rescue. One was during an interview, and I knew I must not accept the job on offer. I never saw an angel or bright lights, or heard sounds, but I know deep inside that the hand belongs to my guardian angel, whom I feel sure will always be at my shoulder.'

The coast of California is very beautiful, especially north of San Francisco, and it was here that Tim had a very lucky escape. Tim and his family were staying with his aunt and uncle for two weeks' holiday. Everyone was having a wonderful time, and Tim especially enjoyed riding in his uncle's motor-boat. Living in land-locked Idaho, the ocean held a real fascination for him, and he could not get into the boat quickly enough.

One morning, his enthusiasm got the better of him, and while everyone else was still eating breakfast, he sneaked outside and climbed into the boat. To this day, no one understands how he managed it, but having watched his uncle intently each day, he had a good idea of how to start the boat. To everyone's horror, they heard the boat spring into life, as the engine roared. The entire household ran outside, to see the boat pull away from the jetty. The boat had been securely moored so it could not go far, but it did rear up alarmingly and hurl Tim into the air.

Tim's mother screamed loudly as he shot upwards, but then, bewilderingly, he did not fall backwards into the water, but came down sideways and landed gently on his feet, right in the middle of the jetty. First he was hugged, and then received a thorough telling off for being so mischievous. Eventually, everyone tried to work out exactly how he had managed to land on the jetty. The air was still, so he could not have been blown there, and it seemed unlikely that a seven-year-old would have been capable of such a leap. On being questioned, Tim said that he had felt hands lift him and place him slowly down again. Everyone thought this explanation quite preposterous, and the debate continued for many years.

Today, however, Tim's mother believes those hands holding Tim belonged to angels, and that he had experienced an angelic rescue.

Julie is a young lady for whom the angels have always been near. Her story concerns the need for protection, and on this occasion no angels, lights, or voices feature. Julie and her mother, however, are convinced that Julie's guardian angel was with her.

Julie is now 22 years of age, but has been aware of the presence of angels since childhood. She recalls as a child seeing small spheres of light, so bright she could scarcely look at them. These balls of light would zoom into her bedroom, where they became transformed into beings of light, watching over her while she fell into a peaceful sleep. Her mother is convinced that Julie's guardian angel is always with her, and she herself has on occasion seen angels. The following story illustrates this point vividly.

Julie was two or three years old and was outside her house with her mother one morning. Her mother went inside just for a moment and Julie was left in the care of some older children. When her mother returned, she was distraught to discover that Julie had disappeared. It transpired that Julie had been abducted by a 13-year-old girl. Her mother, in great distress, called the police, who initiated a search. They were joined by neighbours and friends, and together they spread out over a wide area looking for Julie.

Eventually, after many anxious hours, Julie was found. To everyone's astonishment, she was sitting perfectly still on the edge of a main road, traffic thundering past less than a yard away. She was completely unharmed and calm. Her mother describes her as appearing to have a shield around her. The panic of the day subsided, and her mother and neighbours reflected on the terrible tragedy that might have been. With the knowledge that Julie has now of all the angelic contact in her life, there can be no explanation for her safety that day other than her guardian angel being with her and protecting her.

Swedenborg wrote about angels from a Christian perspective, but was anxious to see the value of different ways of finding God. He acknowledged the varying nature of the individual's personal quest. Many people have had angelic experiences without any religious background whatsoever. Angels are not restricted by race, religion or creed of any kind. With this in mind, it is interesting to come across a story in which someone states, 'I am not a Christian,' as Leah does when describing what happened to her as a five-year-old girl. Even so, the experience has had a profound effect on her life.

'One evening, I was dancing for my parents to some favourite music, when I slipped and fell quite heavily, twisting my ankle badly in the fall. "Bed is the place to be," my father said. "Rest will bring down the swelling." He carried me upstairs and placed me gently in my bed. The bed was quite high and he tucked me in securely and wished me goodnight.

It was very cold, and during the night, as I tossed and turned, the bedclothes fell to the floor. I would normally have woken, shivering and in lots of pain from my ankle, but remarkably I did not. I slept warm and peacefully, and recall a most wonderful dream, full of feelings of love and happiness.

'I woke to find it morning. I sat up in bed and there, sitting at the bottom of my bed in broad daylight, was my guardian angel. I knew instantly why I had felt love and protection. Although only a child, I had no feelings of fear, indeed it all felt perfectly normal. I was definitely not hallucinating, being wide awake in the full light of day.

'The figure was brightly outlined, with a well defined head, neck and shoulders, but the body tapered away. Radiating from the figure was an intense white-yellow light, amazingly bright, but it did not hurt my eyes at all. I gazed in wonder for approximately ten seconds before the angel started to fade. I knew instinctively that I had been protected all night from the cold and the pain of my injury. It was not a life-threatening situation, but my angel did help me nonetheless.

'I know without doubt that what I saw was a spiritual presence, so very real for those few seconds – like another person in the room. It is as fresh and clear in my memory today as on that night so long ago. I am not a Christian, nor do I wish to be, but this experience has definitely made me hold an unshakeable belief in an "afterlife". We should all aim to think of each other as spiritual beings and treat our fellow men with love, kindness and respect. A powerful lesson for life was taught to me that night as a small child.'

Many of the reports of angel experiences today are confusing as to their meaning. Not all are rescues or healing visits, and children are often not able to rationalise their experiences.

Di's angel appeared 82 years ago, but at the time she thought of her simply as a lovely lady. It was not until many years later that she thought of this visitor as an angel, and still does not quite understand why she appeared to her.

Di's story begins in a small hamlet in Dorset, England, called Adber. She lived with her parents and two sisters, who were then 11 and 13 years old, while Di was just four. Their house was very old and large, with many spacious rooms, and an unusual feature: a wide passage running from the rear of the house straight through to the front. This passage was kept clear of furniture to enable the carrying of coal, water and food to the main rooms of the house. The main living-room contained a large open fireplace, with gravel irons attached to the sides to facilitate the hanging and holding of saucepans, and a large hook for the water kettles. The water kettle was made of iron, very large and heavy even when empty. All the water for the house was supplied by a pump situated at the back of the house within a very large kitchen. The children had the task of filling the kettle from the pump, the elder two carrying it, and if it needed refilling after dark, Di had to accompany them carrying a candle. The house had no gas or electricity, so a large supply of candles was essential.

One evening, just after dark, the kettle needed to be filled. It was so heavy that it was necessary for two pairs of hands to lift and carry it along the corridor. Di, as usual, accompanied them with a large, brightly burning candle to light the long, dark passage.

They had arrived at the door of the living-room, when Di cried out in amazement, 'Oh, look!' So loudly had she shouted that her two sisters dropped the kettle, spilling the water and knocking the candle from Di's hands. They could see nothing. She pointed again and asked them, 'Please look.' Scared, they ran to their parents in the living-room, leaving Di alone in the dark passage.

Unafraid, she gazed in wonder at a lovely lady. The lady was shining and glowing in a long silvery dress and a veil. She stood within the glow, a beautiful smile on her face. She lifted a hand, with one finger pointing towards Di, who still felt no fear. The vision faded, and Di was jolted back to earth by the stern voice of her father shouting at her sisters for being so clumsy. Never before had she heard him so angry, and she silently slipped into a nook by the chimney corner out of the way. She believed she must have done something very wrong and remembers feeling almost petrified by this scene.

Di kept the details of what she had seen to herself for years, until at the age of 12 she told her mother. Her mother told her that she had seen a vision. Di has never forgotten the experience. Every detail is still very clear and she feels, whatever explanation people may place upon it, that angels are always near to young children.

I think of the next account as a trio of angels. Remarkably, two children and their mother have been helped by angels, seeing them independently of each other. The mother's story is told first, following by Rebekah's and David's experiences.

Grace is a mother of three children living in North Wales. Her life is now happy and peaceful, but it was not always so. When her third baby was born, to her great distress her husband decided to leave. Emotionally it was an enormous struggle being delivered of a beautiful, healthy baby but without a husband at such a time of need. Caring for a new-born baby in addition to two other small children was extremely strenuous, and Grace felt each day take its toll. She grew weaker physically and mentally, until one day, reaching the end of her strength, she was quite at a loss as to what to do next. That night, sleep would not come. She was in such turmoil and every movement seemed like a huge effort. By the early hours of the morning, in despair, she rang some understanding and supportive friends who dashed round to comfort her. As the husband and wife were Christians, they did the only thing they could at that time which was to pray for Grace. Her friend decided to read Psalm 3, which describes a shield and 'the lifter up of mine head'. At this point,

Grace recalls, two white hands appeared under her face and lifted it, bringing a feeling of lightness and producing a glow. Her friends were both in front of her, so Grace knew that these must be the hands of an angel. The light seemed both to be flowing around her and to be coming from within her heart. From that moment life slowly improved.

A few years passed and although most of the time Grace coped and felt stronger, there were still the inevitable periods of despair. Once again, at a moment of mental and physical exhaustion, Grace was helped. After taking the children to school one morning and watching them run through the school gates, she felt so exhausted and fearful she could not move a muscle. She wondered what would become of her and her children if she could no longer cope. Despondency felt like a cloak of iron, pinning her to the car seat. Knowing prayer had helped her before in such a situation, she started to pray. Suddenly she heard a voice, telling her to get out of the car, walk around the outside of the school and pray for the children. She protested strongly that she had not a grain of energy and found even the idea of leaving the car exhausting, let alone walking around the grounds. Three times in all, the voice instructed her to leave the car, until plucking up her courage and every last remaining ounce of strength, she forced herself to get out of the car and began to walk slowly around the school field.

Suddenly, she felt literally uplifted; a force of energy

was supporting her, flowing with tremendous force from behind her. Turning round, she saw a huge angel dressed as if for battle with breastplate, armour and sword. Light and power radiated from this enormous figure and Grace felt love, energy and hope filling and supporting her. At this point, she became aware that behind this dramatic angel was a vast army stretching as far as the eye could see, all dressed alike in breast-plates and armour. The vision eventually faded, but the sensations of love, support and especially of energy remained. Grace found her life completely changed from that moment on. The knowledge that the angels were there to help and sustain her had given Grace the will and the strength to go forward happily. She was not at all surprised then, by the following events concerning her children.

Rebekah lay on her bed one night but not yet asleep. Suddenly she became aware that something was happening in the room. Sitting up, she saw four beautiful angels appear, one in each corner of the bedroom, hovering above the ground and radiating light. They were dressed in long white gowns, and had shimmering, almost translucent wings. Rebekah was totally at ease and unafraid, feeling only happiness at such a wonderful sight, a powerful symbol of care and love for a nine-year-old little girl.

David is ten years old, and he told me about this encounter with an angel recently, only months after it happened. He was unsure why, but for several years he had worried about dying. The fear had increased with time until it was becoming a great burden, not only to himself but to his family. Talking and trying to reassure him seemed ineffective and Grace reasoned that since prayer had changed her life, special prayers for David might be the answer. After talking to their minister, it was agreed that David should be prayed for in church.

One evening David went to the front of the church, standing before the altar where the minister and a lady member were to pray for him. They prayed that David would be released from this awful fear. As they prayed, an angel appeared by David's side, shining and dressed in a bright yellow robe. He was unsure as to whether the angel had wings, but it had a lovely, kind face. Reaching out, the angel took his hand and immediately they were in a place beyond the church. David saw a beautiful pastoral scene, with green fields and cows peacefully grazing. The angel said, 'This is heaven, David. There is nothing to be afraid of – it's perfectly lovely.' David gazed at the wonderful landscape and felt his fear evaporate. Then they were in the church once more, with the angel still holding his hand. The brightness was intense, but his eyes could easily cope with the light; it did not hurt at all. The angel released his hand and slowly faded from sight, leaving David happy and unafraid. David saw the lady in the church who had been praying with the minister staring at him in astonishment, for she too had seen the angel.

David is now a happy and contented ten-year-old,

his fear of death and dying completely gone. He told me in a very matter-of-fact way all about his experience. These three members of one family were all helped in different ways by three very different angel experiences.

6

The Last Goodnight

With silence only as their benediction God's angels come,
Where, in the shadow of a great affliction, the soul sits dumb.

JOHN GREENLEAF WHITTIER

Accounts of the increasing number of experiences reported by many people who come close to death are now well-known. One of the most striking and life-changing elements, which is frequently encountered in these NDEs is the 'being of light'. This links up strongly in several ways with some of the angelic experiences included in this book. Some of these similarities or connections may well help us to understand what is being experienced in these situations.

People often find it hard to describe their contact with the being of light. Some describe it as a 'living light', others report a feeling of warmth radiating internally and externally. Raymond Moody, in his book *Life After Life*, tells of one person's experience as like talking to somebody, but without there being an actual person there. This combination of personal contact and light is clearly akin to angelic experiences, including angels who appear in connection with death, as we shall see.

The experiences people have of angels are often linked to crises, and the approach of death is a crisis in which one might expect angels to be involved. As messengers, they can bridge the gap between this world and the next.

Light and angels, therefore, are often connected with people close to death, but what of the loved ones left behind? Are they, too, helped by the angels to overcome their grief? In many cases the answer is yes. It may be a brilliant light, as previously discussed, containing the feeling of a presence and radiating comfort, or it may also be the person who has died reappearing in angel form.

Judith badly needed reassurance that she was not as isolated and alone as she felt after a bereavement, and eventually she found it.

'My parents met on a boat while emigrating to Australia from England in 1965 and married in Sydney. My mother was from Preston in Lancashire and when I was a child spent many hours talking about her childhood. We planned to visit one day, but as the years passed, with no plans to travel to England, I thought it was just a dream that would never be realised. To my amazement, when I was 23 years old, my mother announced that we were to visit England at Christmas.

There were several family celebrations to be held at this time, and we were being urged to make an effort to come to the reunion.

'We arrived in Preston, which was very cold. The welcome, however, was as warm as toast. My mother was very happy and, although for some time she had been suffering from angina, she was determined to enjoy her visit to the full. We had a lovely time, and as our departure date drew nearer, we began to feel sad. The Saturday night before our Tuesday morning flight, it was agreed that we should all go out to a local hotel for a farewell dinner. Thirty family members and friends gathered and it was a night to remember.

'The following morning my mother complained of feeling unwell, but decided against seeking medical help. Instead, she used the tablets she always had with her for attacks of angina. The pain, however, increased during the day, until by evening my aunt insisted on calling an ambulance. I sat beside my mother, holding her hand all the way to the hospital, but despite every effort on our arrival, she died an hour later. I was devastated. We had been much closer than mother and daughter. We had been best friends, and I couldn't imagine life without her.

'After these events, my memory is a blur. She was buried in a family grave in her beloved Lancashire, and I flew home to Sydney alone, completely bereft. My father had died when I was twelve years old and so I returned to an empty flat. Friends and colleagues were very supportive, but somehow I could not get my life back together. I could not shake off the terrible feelings of loss.

'One night, a year after I had returned to Australia, I was at my lowest ebb. I paced the flat, crying, desperate for something to take the pain away. As I turned towards the kitchen worktop to pour myself a drink, I became aware of the light in the room becoming tremendously bright. I turned around and there in front of me was my mother – as real as if she were solid flesh and blood! On either side of her stood an angel, with piercing blue eyes and huge white wings. All three figures were approximately one foot above the ground. I felt no fear – just a marvellous feeling of comfort and love. The angels' wings fanned forwards, as if to embrace me, and my mother smiled, radiating love.

'Seconds later they faded, but I was left elated, healed and very comforted. I now know for certain that death is not the end, and that my mother is ever near, watching, guiding and loving me as always. I still miss her, and always will, but that night changed my life. I am once more a happy, confident person with everything to look forward to.'

We have already met Paniyota and her sister Vaghoulla, who used to wave goodnight to the cherubs on her way to bed. This year Paniyota saw an angel herself. This second story about the family has many similarities with what we have just heard from Judith. It takes place much later in the sisters' lives, after they and their brothers had come to live in England. Paniyota now lives in north London and for a long time she had been very worried about her mother, who still lived in the same village in Cyprus. She had been ill, so Paniyota had made several journeys back to Cyprus. Paniyota's mother died in February 1995, and the family all gathered on Cyprus for the funeral. The funeral took place on a Thursday and it was hard to say goodbye. Paniyota was terribly distressed by the events of the previous few years and the eventual loss of her mother.

Friday dawned clear and bright. Paniyota decided she had to be alone, to walk, be quiet and seek solace in the countryside. Walking into the fields, she felt the need to meditate and calm her mind. Closing her eyes, she tried to clear her mind of the worry she was feeling. Suddenly, in front of her stood her mother. Her feet were not touching the ground and she hovered about a foot above the grass. She was dressed in a long, pale-blue gown, and had two furled white wings. No words were spoken, but Paniyota knew at once by the smile on her face and by the light radiating from her that she was happy and free from pain in heaven. The relief that flooded through her at this wonderful sight was truly marvellous. The peace she had so longed for came over her. Twice more since this occasion during times of meditation Paniyota's mother has appeared to her as an angel. It is Paniyota's fervent hope that she may continue to appear to her, but she has the peace of mind of knowing that her mother is happy in the life beyond this.

Seeing angels is less about outer reality and more about our inner state. We might even call this a visionary state. This does not, however, make the angels any less real; it means the experience is anchored at a much deeper level. We are opening our spiritual eyes and awareness. Swedenborg defines this inner or higher level of consciousness as people's 'angelic part'. Maybe when death is close we see angels because we are in touch with this deeper spiritual level, and see through our own 'angel eyes'.

This could explain why, when Betty visited a friend at the point of death, she could not see what her sick friend clearly could. She recalls her visit in the summer of 1995 as follows:

'Last year a dear friend who had been unwell for some 12 months was diagnosed as suffering from terminal cancer. As her physical condition worsened, her spirit and positive response to life and people never wavered. Indeed, by contrast, it became clearer and a source of inspiration to the many friends who visited her.

'As our annual holiday approached, she was becoming physically ever weaker, and we prayed that she would still be with us on our return. Two weeks later, as my husband arranged to visit her, he was warned that her condition had rapidly deteriorated as she had become unable to take either food or liquid. During my husband's visit, it was arranged that I would go and sit with her a couple of days later, while her husband and daughter went out to attend to some urgent matters. By this time visitors were being reduced to a minimum, so I was grateful to have this opportunity to be with her for a while. My husband confirmed that there was indeed a dramatic change in her appearance, and again came the warning not to be taken aback by it.

'When the day for my visit arrived, I became increasingly fearful in case shock at her appearance should register on my face and so upset her. As I left home, I felt impelled to turn back to draw a card from a set of texts I have from a spiritual teaching. Usually I cut the stack of over 250 cards, but as I took them from the box, they slipped from my hands and fell on to the table, fanning out into a large semicircle with just one sticking out of line. That was the card I chose. I was so moved by the words that my fear fell away and I was able to go forward in a positive state of love. In such a sad situation it may seem strange to say that the time I spent with my friend was a wonderful experience — just standing beside her bed, holding hands, talking very little. Her hands felt remarkably strong that day, and when she did speak it was never of herself, nor had she lost her sense of humour. Somehow the atmosphere seemed "golden"; fear and sadness were dispelled, and all I was aware of was the peace and serenity of her spirit.

'When her daughter returned a couple of hours later, my friend stirred and, looking sideways towards the settee, asked, "Who is that sitting there?" As I was the only other person in the room, her daughter answered, "It's Betty." Her mother said in a clear voice, "No, I know Betty's here, but someone else has been there looking on the whole time."

'Now, I believe in angels, and I know that her daughter believes in angels too. A look of understanding passed between us. We both accepted that her mother was able to see what we with our physical eyes could not see. But, I had certainly experienced a heavenly presence and atmosphere during my visit.

'Three days later, my friend passed into the spiritual world. Her heart was so pure and her hands felt so strong – she is surely well on her way to angelhood.'

This next moving story also describes seeing with spiritual eyes as the moment of death approached. This person believed that everyone in the room must have been able to see the vision revealed to him. The story is told by Ian, who was living in Sydney at the time, and was the minister to this close and happy family. It is an occasion he will never forget.

'I well remember the phone call when the young wife told me her husband and the father of their three young children had been diagnosed as having terminal cancer. I also remember the day of his death. I remember the atmosphere and the waiting – waiting until he sent a message for me to come in. He told me how close "it" now was. He talked, mostly with his eyes closed, of the farewells he had made and the ends he had tied up and finished with. But he was so tired. He seemed to just want to rest, have peace of mind and be out of it. The fight was over now.

'A nurse was in the room with us and she turned on a music tape, which he had often listened to as a way of helping him deal with pain. Gone now was the paraphernalia of drips and life support systems. Tears streaming down her face, his wife knelt by the bed, cradling his head in her arms. She talked to him softly, reassuring him when restless. Then, surprising us all, he half sat up, eyes wide open, reaching forward to the end of the bed. "The little children," he said, "do you see them?" "Yes, darling," his wife cried, "we can see them." Filled with an indescribably different atmosphere now, the room became a place of peace and acceptance. In our hearts we willed his death and release. The angels had, we knew, come to help and welcome him.

'Sinking back into the pillows, a shadow of pain passed across his face before he let go and allowed the love and welcome of the angels to envelop him, their childlike appearance having comforted and reassured him not many minutes before. It was an unforgettable privilege to experience the presence of angels, so powerfully felt in this extraordinary way.'

Descriptions of angels vary considerably. Often they are seen as very large. Janet's experience tells of an angel, who was enormous, and yet she felt no fear. Janet's family has a strong faith, which has clearly deepened through this incident.

In the summer of 1995 the condition of Janet's husband Bob, who had been ill for two years, started to deteriorate rapidly. During this time Bob and Janet were sustained by their faith, having been Christians for many years. Bob's courage was strong, but as his condition worsened and the ordeal started to drain him more and more, he knew that it was time to leave and he prayed to be released from his illness.

One day Janet was so weary that she too prayed for help. Seeing how distressed and tired her mother was, Janet's daughter begged her to go and sleep for a short while at least. Dreading not being awake should Bob need her, Janet fought the idea, but was eventually persuaded to lie down and try to rest. Knowing that her body longed to do this, she went upstairs to the bedroom and lay down beside her husband, ensuring that she was able to hear should he need her.

Stretching out, she tried to relax. Suddenly, a feeling of pure peace swept over her and she became aware of a figure standing at the end of the bed. Unafraid, she gazed, transfixed, at a man with bright yellow hair. His face was a little hazy and ill defined, but he wore a red breastplate and carried a sword in his hand. His arms were large and muscular and appeared tanned, but his face was pale and translucent and seemed bathed with light from within. All of a sudden, Janet started to realise how enormous this figure was, taller than the room itself, for his head touched the ceiling and his feet looked to be below the level of the floor. The whole corner of the room was filled with this gigantic figure.

Janet lay watching him, but was aware that he looked only at Bob, with great intensity. She ran from the room, burning to share this experience with some-one. Later her daughter said she could tell by the expression on her mother's face and the luminescence of her eyes that something quite extraordinary had taken place. 'I've seen an angel,' she told her daughter, and it was clear that she had witnessed something of God. Very shortly after these events, Bob died. There is a wonderful consolation, however, in knowing that he is at peace and, to use Janet's words, 'The Lord sent a special angel to watch over him, then to hold his hand and take him home.'

Natalie had never been strong. Since early child-hood she had suffered from asthma and during the cold New York winters would frequently succumb to bronchitis. The doctor told her parents that the best possible help would be a warm dry cli-mate. Money was scarce, however, and though her parents worked hard and saved, it took many years before they were able to move to America's West Coast. Eventually, when Natalie was 16 years old, they moved to Pasadena in California. The family settled well, content with their new life, and initially Natalie's health was greatly improved.

Natalie married and produced two sons, but despite the dry atmosphere she was still plagued by respiratory problems. When the boys had left home and her husband was approaching retirement, they decided to move once more to the 'high desert' of Yucca Valley. She enjoyed many years in the Valley, but discovered one day that her breathing was deteriorating and that she would need a hospital appointment. This time the news was worse than ever: lung cancer, and Natalie did not have much time left. The news was met with stoicism. She took to spending more and more time in the garden, even sleeping there and feeling very close to nature. She took great pleasure in the night sky, huge bright stars piercing the black of the desert sky.

On one of these nights she called her husband to come and look at the sky. She pointed out a bright, blue-white light among the stars, and asked if he knew what it was. Her husband could see only stars and looked puzzled. She said the light was growing in size until it seemed to fill her immediate view of the sky and assumed the shape of a figure. Her husband tried to rationalise this by saying it might be some natural phenomenon brought about by unusual weather conditions. However, the weather was normal, and he could see nothing untoward in the sky. Natalie gazed in awe, and was clearly very happy with the sight she described.

Her husband returned indoors to answer the telephone. Discovering it was one of his sons, he told him what his mother had said. Both were puzzled, but dismissed it. Finishing the phone call, Natalie's husband went into the kitchen to pour them both a cool drink. He then sat down on the chair next to Natalie, and turned to hand her the drink. She had gone, still staring up at the night sky with a peaceful, happy expression on her face.

Several of the stories presented here describe the pain of loss when a loved one dies and the comfort of seeing the loved one again in angel form. Adults may struggle terribly with grief at this time, but children also feel a sense of isolation and desertion. Mary found the loss of her father unbearable. His appearance to her after death was vital in giving her strength to carry on.

'I loved my father dearly, but when I was just ten years old I learned he was suffering from a terminal illness. He struggled with his illness for three long years, until everybody was wishing him a blessed release. After he died, I became engulfed by a sense of loss and loneliness. I didn't realise at 13 years of age that this was depression. I even wished that I could die, to be with my father once more and feel happy. I was full of unresolved anger, feeling angry towards everything and everybody. This persisted for quite some time, but came to an end one particular night, the memory of which will remain with me for ever.

'Despite all my problems, I always managed to sleep, but one night, in the early hours of the morning, I was woken by the sound of my name being called. I sat up in bed and there, standing in the bedroom doorway, was my father. He was not as I had last seen him, ill and gaunt. He looked exactly as he had before his illness; his face had a pink, healthy glow, and his auburn hair was neatly combed. He was dressed in his uniform, having worked for the local bus company, "Ribble Motors". As in life, his boots shone, his shirt was white, and his tie neatly tied; the only thing missing was his hat. My most vivid memory is of the expression of joy and peace on his face. I distinctly remember shouting the word "Daddy", and I was rewarded with the most wonderful smile imaginable. Joy, peace and happiness radiated around the room, and I felt transfixed for what seemed like ages.

'Eventually, with a gentle nod of his head, my father began to walk slowly backwards out of the room. After this, I knew he was happy and free from pain, and although I still cried for many weeks afterwards, I became reconciled to his death. I know in my heart that this was a celestial experience. I believe my guardian angel looks after me, and had arranged this visit and made it possible for me to see my father once more.

'My second experience involves my mother. She died very suddenly on 14 February 1981. She had taken my two sons to the seaside town of Southport. After returning to her house after their day out, my mother rang to say that they were home and well, and had had a wonderful time. It was arranged that I would collect them the following morning. At this time I was working as a barmaid in a local residential hotel, and at about 11.30 that night, when I was busy clearing everything away, I received a phone call. It was from one of my sons, saying that my mother did not feel well, and asking me to come immediately. My colleagues took over and I drove to my mother's home.

'On arrival I found my mother sitting in her usual fireside chair and looking for all the world as though she were peacefully asleep. But she could not be roused, so, covering her with a blanket, I immediately called for an ambulance. Again my world was turned upside down, but at this point I started to recall a vision or message that had entered my head some months before. In this vision I was told how my mother's funeral was to be arranged, which of my brothers and sisters were to read lessons, and what part my own sons and daughters and myself had to play in the requiem mass for my mother. I had had this vision several months before my mother's death, and at the time felt horror and shame. At this time, my mother was healthy, working and enjoying an active social life with her friends and grandchildren.

'However, this was not the only strange thing that had happened around that time. Calling at my mother's house one day shortly after I had had the vision, I found her carefully wrapping her precious china, and packing it into boxes. When I asked her why she was doing this, she replied, "I've a feeling I'll be leaving here soon." I concluded that she had finally decided to move to a smaller house nearer me, a suggestion I had made many times. That Christmas and New Year were among the happiest we had spent together and this is still a wonderful consolation to me.

'After her death, the funeral arrangements were carried out exactly as I had been instructed. I truly believe that without those details and the forewarning I could not have coped. Although some people might not see the involvement of the angels in these incidents, I believe that yet again my celestial guardian angel was protecting me. There have been other episodes since, which continue to convince me of this, including a dream in which my mother appeared to me and reassured me about my brother, who was seriously ill at the time. Even though I was still distressed afterwards, I soon felt comforted and knew that this was another example of my being helped by my angel.'

For Dorothea too, seeing a person who had died was a source of comfort and strength. She felt 16 December 1984 would be a fairly ordinary Sunday, and that is how it began. In the afternoon, she and George, her husband, decided to visit their holiday house by the sea. Their two children, Jane and James, then aged 15 and 11, chose to stay at home in order to complete their homework. It was unusual for them to be apart during weekends, but, after all, Dorothea and George would only be gone for a few hours. After an hour's journey, they arrived at the small seaside town on the east coast of England, and took their usual walk along the beach, returning to the house to sit by the fire with tea and biscuits and the Sunday newspapers. Dorothea continues.

'After a little while George set aside his newspaper, came to me with outstretched arms, enveloped me in a hug and kissed me tenderly. This was to be our last embrace, for within an instant and without another word George had collapsed and died from a massive brain haemorrhage. In a flash, as I held him in my arms, I had the distinct feeling that George was now somewhere else and what I was left holding on to was only a shell.'

This in itself is not an angelic experience but what happened next was.

'The days immediately following were spent contacting relatives and friends, receiving visitors and trying to come to terms with what had happened. During this time the children and I were sleeping together each night, so that we would be close to comfort one another. One night, I was awakened by a brilliant light entering the room. As I sat up and looked towards the light, I saw an amazing sight. There was George, arms by his side, with the palms of his hands held out towards me. His long gown was of the most intense blue I had ever seen. His skin gleamed, and his face held an expression of such joy and peace that the memory remains with me, as fresh as if it were yesterday.'

There have been many experiences of light in the accounts in this book. Some people are in no doubt that the brilliance of this light and the accompanying feelings can only be the results of an angelic presence. Others are reluctant to attach any label to the experience, but it remains clear and awesome in their minds. Is the 'being of light' a personal angel, which provides a communication with or even a portrayal of God? Or is it even possible that we see God through these shining forms and light? People certainly speak of a presence, but we cannot describe the phenomenon objectively or with absolute precision, given that it is so charged with personal significance and emotion.

Certainly, this was the case for Stella. She was very close to her sister Marjory, who lived in Melbourne, Australia. Marjory was married with a family and lived a happy life in the sunshine, away from the cold and damp of Manchester. At this time Stella was unmarried, living at home in Manchester with others in her family. Her bedroom was at the back of the house, overlooking the golf course. She was always aware of just how quiet and dark it was at night. No street lights and no car headlights could penetrate the dark of the golf course.

It was therefore with great astonishment that one night, in the early hours of the morning, Stella awoke to find her bedroom filled with light, intense and glowing, accompanied by the powerful sensation of a presence. Warmth and love radiated from the light, as well as calmness and reassurance. She was unafraid and full of wonder, knowing there could be no natural explanation. The days to follow brought great sadness, for the family received the news that Marjory had died. This was devastating, not least because of their concern for Marjory's husband and young family. Eventually, they received the coroner's report. It was then that Stella realised the significance of her experience, for Marjory had died at the exact moment that, half a world away, Stella's bedroom had filled with a presence and bright light.

Nurses are frequently described as angels and several years ago a TV series about nurses was entitled *Angels*. Carers of all types are often put into this category. We have suggested elsewhere that humans have an angelic part within and are capable of higher levels of consciousness. Some people seem to be more open to this aspect of themselves and are more able to let it flow out into the world. We all have opportunities to be angels of mercy, but in some cases these opportunities are heightened. The first part of this final story, which Peter shares with us, is about angelic gifts being transmitted into a situation of suffering through a very human man.

'My eldest son Robert was diagnosed with terminal childhood cancer at the age of five in July 1975. He did well on chemotherapy treatment for many months, and we were introduced to spiritual healing via the famous healer Harry Edwards. Robert only had one appointment with Harry, but I corresponded with him weekly. Most of Harry's work was done as absent or distant healing. It seemed to work very well. Every problem brought to Harry's attention seemed to disappear or miraculously improve by the time we received Harry's next letter. Even Robert's fear of hospital treatment suddenly disappeared. Was there really some link between Harry and Robert via a source of healing or angelic influence, or was it just coincidence, as the drugs held the illness at bay? Certainly, it seemed like the latter, when in April 1976 the illness began to spread rapidly, so that Robert was wracked with pain, which no medicine was able to contain any more.

'Robert was on the highest permitted dose of morphine and yet spent much of the time screaming with pain. My wife Barbara and I were at our wits' end. It was Barbara's birthday on 2 July and, amidst all the suffering, I had forgotten to buy a present. "You know that all I want is a miracle," she said. In fact, I was contemplating the opposite. I thought that the only way out was to take his life by overdosing with morphine – I was truly desperate. Then came a knock on the door. A young man was standing there, who said he was a healer and could heal any condition. He had heard of our plight through friends of our next-door neighbour. We invited him in, but even his confidence drained a little when he saw Robert's pitiful condition. He lay like a little skeleton, having not eaten for about ten days.

'The healer, who was 20 years old and whose name was Tony, administered healing from his hands, using water as an intermediary. I held a bucket of warm water, while Tony moved his hands around the bucket, as if projecting energy into it. He never touched the water or the bucket, but we would then pour the water from the bucket into the bath. We half-filled the bath in this way and laid Robert in the water. He was distressed so we only held him in it for a couple of minutes, but when we laid him on the bed his pain was gone. We could touch and dry his limbs without him screaming. He said, "That water came into me." I was grateful, but didn't really expect the effect to be permanent, so I gave Robert some more pain-killing medicine before he went to bed. That was the last medicine he had during the remaining two months of his life. During that night, he woke up only to ask for food, and ate ravenously several times. The colour came back to his cheeks. He was permanently free of pain, although the consultants at Great Ormond Street Children's Hospital in London insisted on having him in for observation before accepting that this was so.

'The healing and bathing treatment continued and the tumours were visibly shrinking, but unfortunately Robert was no longer able to produce his own blood; he was dependent on regular blood transfusions. His own blood-producing cells had been irreparably damaged by the illness and the medical treatment. However, his quality of life was transformed. His last two months of life were relatively comfortable, and he was able to take an active interest in life. For this we are eternally grateful and thank God for sending Tony in our hour of need – he was our angel in human form.

'When Robert did die, in the early morning of 26 August 1976, it was unexpected. Some of the circumstances surrounding his death suggested in retrospect to us that maybe there had been a different sort of angelic input involved. He was in Great Ormond Street Hospital having a blood transfusion, following a meeting the day before with the medical team, who had acknowledged the achievement of the healer and agreed to continue with the routine of blood transfusions as long as we wished. We had left him in the care of the nurses for the night, and returned home for some sleep, as was our custom by then. At about 6 a.m, the phone began to make peculiar tinkling noises, as if engineers were tinkering with the line, or as if the bell was being blown by the wind – but the weather was hot and still. Eventually, after half an hour of this inter-mittent tinkling, which disturbed our sleep, the phone rang properly. It was the night sister from Great Ormond Street. "Whatever is wrong with your tele-phone?" she said. "I've been trying to ring you for the last half-hour. Robert is slipping away from us. You must come straightaway."

'We hastily took the other two children next door and made the half-hour drive to the hospital – but we were half an hour too late, he had gone. The phone never repeated its tricks – it never needed to be fixed. Why did this happen at that time to prevent us from being with our son in his final moments on this earth? At the time it seemed cruel, but with hindsight we realised that we had not been ready to let him go; our presence would have held him back. Also, we would have undoubtedly taken Tony with us to try and keep him alive, which would have been inappropriate. But what a learning experience for us -the realisation that at the point of leaving this world there is a force at work, which takes charge of the process, can override our telephone system, and chooses who should be at the bedside. The angel of death is not the "grim reaper", but a kindly, benevolent being, who takes appropriate action to lead the new arrival gently into the spiritual world. Over the years, the realisation that Robert was not alone in death, but was being cared for, has meant more to me than the immediate regret of not being there to hold his hand when he passed away.'

In conclusion, it is clear that angels are woven into our culture, and that they are part of the fabric of religions world-wide. They act as 'guardians' not just to individuals but to institutions, places, nations, even skills or crafts. They predate the Bible by many years, and it seems that as long as there have been people, there have been angel experiences.

There will always be a debate as to whether angels have human origins or whether they are a race apart, who have never lived on earth. I believe that their ability to empathise with our predicaments suggests that they have had human experience themselves. For years they have baffled scientists, who want to account for them in material terms (or not at all) on the physical plane. Even in this realm, however, a sense of something 'other' has been growing. For example, rumours abound of astronauts seeing angels on their space missions.

As we approach the millennium, could it be that we are once more looking to the future with spiritual eyes? Are we ready to acknowledge that not everything can be explained by science, valuable though it may be? Could we all be being constantly 'affected' by angels, whether we know it or not? Swedenborg believed our lives are lived not just in the company of our fellow humans on earth, but also in the midst of people who are now in the other world, and that their influence is reaching us all the time. Do they help us with decisions? How often do we have a thought and think, 'Where did that come from?' Jean, whose moving account on the narrowboat is recorded earlier, firmly believes that if we want our angel to help, we only have to ask. She has often called upon hers, and always receives a response. Ask yours to come into your life, and you may be very surprised at the result!

7

How to contact your guardian angel

As these stories have shown us, all kinds of people have had angelic encounters – men, women and children from all walks of life, all over the world. Most of them are normal people leading ordinary lives; they are not priests, saints or mystics. The experiences have nearly always happened spontaneously, often triggered by a crisis or great need but sometimes for no obvious reason at all. Some people have had many experiences of angels and are aware of their presence all the time. This is particularly the case with children, but children often lose touch with their angels as they grow up, partly because of the disbelief of other children or adults.

People who see angels all the time are not necessarily believers or practitioners of a formal religion, nor more spiritually developed, though they may be more aware of other realms of consciousness and have other kinds of experiences of these levels. People who meditate regularly or have a spiritual practice may be more open to such experiences, though this is not necessarily the case. Highly creative people such as artists, musicians and poets may also be in touch with 'higher realms'. William Blake is an example of someone who saw and talked to angels throughout his life and created poems and pictures out of his experiences. Yet such visions may also come to people with no outstanding talents or qualifications.

HOW TO SEE ANGELS

It is often said that seeing is believing. This does not mean that religious belief is a precondition – indeed, it can be a disqualification if it encourages rigidly dogmatic beliefs on the subject. Some people have had their religious faith confirmed by their experiences, but such events happen to believers and non-believers alike. What is important is at least some degree of openness to the dimension of the unknown and mysterious. Children are more likely to see angels because they still possess a capacity for wonder, open eyes and an accepting heart. This is not the same as being naive and gullible, but it does mean not interpreting all phenomena in terms of science and materialism, shutting out whatever does not conform to these theories. If you are willing to accept that reason cannot explain everything, to allow a little mystery into your life, you can become more conscious of subtle signals and promptings from your own intuition and inner voice as well as from beyond.

We are all born with an intuitive capacity, but many of us have this knocked out of us by our education and by learning a system of social values. Yet even if this has been the case, since it is part of our nature, we can all learn to cultivate intuition, listen to and heed its promptings. There are so many stories of lives being saved, disaster averted, by people listening to an inner voice saying, 'Don't travel on that train tomorrow', or 'Go back and check the house again'. The more we learn to respect this voice and listen to it, the stronger and clearer its messages will become. Some people are more visual and see images and visions, while others operate out of feelings and instincts, but it is the same process at work. Some of the stories in this book do not distinguish between the inner voice of intuition and an outer angelic voice, but the two seem to be closely connected and can support each other.

CONTACTING YOUR GUARDIAN ANGEL

It has been strongly suggested by people relating NDEs in this book and elsewhere that angels are very near at death. We are all familiar with the expression 'Angel of Death', and it seems that the 'being of light' encountered in this experience could be this angel who helps us into the next world. Such accounts also frequently describe loved ones in angelic form appearing at the time of death, radiating love and bringing comfort and reassurance through the bright light and familiar form.

As these accounts have revealed, people are frequently helped at the point of death as well as being healed or rescued. But you may well ask, what about me? Do we all have a guardian angel? Are they there all the time, and if so, how can we attain their help? I certainly do not believe that we can summon our guardian angel on demand, but we can ask for help. If we try to be still, angels will come to us.

Meditation and visualisation are good ways of contacting our angels. Find a quiet, peaceful spot, indoors or outdoors, and sit comfortably. If you have a favourite meditation, you can use this. Otherwise just sit still, allow your breathing to be natural and regular and your mind to quieten down. Get in touch with your inner self, the positive, kind and thoughtful side of yourself, which is sometimes called our 'angelic nature'. Angels are all around like radio waves; if we 'tune in' to them, we can become a receiver. Listen, and you may hear words of advice, comfort, wisdom, either aloud or silent like thoughts. If you are a visual type, you may like to allow an image of your angel to form itself in your mind.

Think about events in your life that on reflection you cannot explain. Have you ever felt a hand touch you when alone? Have you instinctively changed your mind about an action that might have led to disastrous consequences if you had gone ahead? Many subtle events may have been your guardian angel intervening in your life without your knowledge.

So invite angels into your life, talk to them and listen to them. You can even write letters to them, asking their help. When they respond, be grateful and thank them. Angels are a neverending fount of love and wisdom, and more is always available. Be open to their presence and their help, and you too can find an angel at your shoulder. You may even find your life is transformed, like so many of the people whose stories are told in this book.

Further Reading

ANGELS AND ANGEL LORE

Chessman, Harriet Scott (ed), *Literary Angels* (Fawcett Columbine/Ballantine, 1994). Angels in the Arts.

Davidson, Gustav, *A Dictionary of Angels* (Free Press, 1971). Exhaustive, well researched survey of angel lore and tradition.

Freeman, Eileen Elias, *Touched by Angels* (HarperCollins, 1994). In-depth contemporary accounts of encounters with angels in the Christian tradition.

Giovetti, Paola, *Angels: the Role of Celestial Guardians and Beings of Light* (Weiser, 1993). Includes Biblical and Christian as well as modern experiences. Also looks at angels in art and contains colour plates.

Graham, Billy, *Angels, God's Secret Agents* (Hodder & Stoughton, 1976). Angels from a traditional Christian perspective.

Israel, Martin, *Angels, Messengers of Grace* (SPCK, 1995). Strong on the Biblical side, but includes healing, psychology and parapsychology.

Kirven, Robert H, *Angels in Action* (Chrysalis, 1994). Swedenborg's views on angels.

Moolenburgh, H C, *A Handbook of Angels* (S W Daniel, 1984). A Dutch doctor presents his patients' experiences of angels.

Ronner, John, *Know Your Angels: The Angel Almanac* (Mamre Press, 1993). Condensed account of the different types of angels.

Swedenborg Emanuel, *Heaven and Hell* (Swedenborg Society, 1989). Also available in an abridged edition, *The Shorter Heaven and Hell* (Seminar Books, 1993).

Taylor, Terry Lynn, *Messengers of Light* (H J Kramer, 1990). Links angels with personal growth.

NEAR-DEATH EXPERIENCES

Eadie, Betty, *Embraced by the Light* (Thorsons, 1994).

Grey, Margot, *Return from Death* (Arkana, 1985).

Moody, Raymond, *Life After Life* (Bantam, 1976).

Morse, Melvin, *Parting Visions* (Piatkus, 1995).

Sutherland, Cherie, *Within the Light* (Bantam, 1993).

Resource Guide

In the course of research for this book I have come across several people who are enthusiastic about taking their interest in angels out to others in a particular way, whether through selling books and other articles, painting or whatever. Here are details of these ventures:

Hazel Raven, Gaia, Unit 19, The Corn Exchange, Manchester M4 3EY. Included in what Hazel sells in her shop are angel cards painted by her daughter, Martyne.

Jean Jael, 1 Cardwell Crescent, Oxford OX3 7QE. Jean Jael paints angels, working from intuition. Cards and originals are available. Please write to her if you are interested, **enclosing an s.a.e.**

The Original Angel Emporium, PO Box 16, Wilmslow, SK9 2NE. This is the first angel mail-order business in Britain, with books, videos, and all sorts of angel items and gifts. Please write to the above address for a catalogue.

The following provide information and publications and run courses or lectures relating to Swedenborg:

New Church College, 25 Radcliffe New Road, Radcliffe, Manchester M26 1LE.

The Swedenborg Movement, c/o 98 Abbotts Drive, Wembley, Middx, HA0 3SQ.

The Swedenborg Society, 20-21 Bloomsbury Way, London WC1A 2TH.

I know of no angel 'networks' or publications dedicated to angels in Britain. The following are details for those which exist in the United States:

The AngelWatch Foundation, PO Box 1397, Mountainside NJ 07092-0397. This provides a bimonthly newsletter and works to raise awareness of angels.

Angel Times, 4360 Chamblee-Dunwoody Road, Ste. 400, Atlanta GA 30341. This is a full-colour magazine which focuses on angels.

If you have had an angel experience and would be willing to share it with the author, please contact her at New Church College, 25 Radcliffe New Road, Radcliffe, Manchester M26 1LE.